In Season and Out of Season:

Sermons to a Nation

In Season and Out of Season:

Sermons to a Nation

David Gitari

Copyright © David Gitari 1996

First published 1996

02 01 00 99 98 97 96 7 6 5 4 3 2 1

Regnum is an imprint of Paternoster Publishing,
P.O. Box 300, Carlisle, Cumbria CA3 0QS, U.K.

The right of David Gitari to be identified as the Author
of this work has been asserted by him in accordance with the
Copyright, Designs and Patents Act 1988.

*All Rights Reserved. No part of this publication may
be reproduced, stored in a retrieval system, or
transmitted in any form or by any means, electronic,
mechanical, photocopying, recording or otherwise,
without the prior permission of the publisher
or a licence permitting restricted copying.
In the U.K. such licences are issued by the
Copyright Licensing Agency, 90 Tottenham Court Road,
London W1P 9HE*

Unless otherwise stated, Scripture quotations in this
publication are from the Holy Bible, New International Version.
Copyright © 1973, 1978, 1984 International Bible Society.
Published by Zondervan and Hodder & Stoughton.

*This book is sold subject to the condition that it shall
not, by way of trade or otherwise be lent, re-sold,
hired out, or otherwise circulated without the
publisher's prior consent in any form of binding or
cover other than that in which it is published and
without a similar condition including this condition
being imposed on the subsequent purchaser.*

British Library Cataloguing in Publication Data

Gitari, David
In season and out of season: sermons to a nation
1.Sermons, English
I.Title
252

ISBN 1–870345–11–8

Typeset by Photoprint, Torquay, Devon
Printed in Great Britain by BPC Wheatons Ltd, Exeter

Contents

Dedication

Dedicated to Grace, Sammy, Jonathan and Mwendwa – members of my immediate family from whom I have learned and shared the ups and downs of life and who gave me courage to prophesy; to all clergy, lay-readers and evangelists who stood in solidarity with me when I preached these prophetic sermons in the days of the Diocese of Mt Kenya East, April 1975 to June 1990; to all my colleagues in the ministry who have continually stood in solidarity with me as I prophesied to the people of Kirinyaga and Kenya during the last four years (July 1990 to June 1994).

Foreword

I met David Gitari twenty years ago, when he was General Secretary of the Pan African Fellowship of Evangelical Students (PAFES). At that time I was also considering which direction my own Christian service should take.

Since those early times, we have been closely associated within the International Fellowship of Evangelical Mission Theologians (INFEMIT), of which he was the founding Chairman, as well as the African Theological Fellowship (ATF), of which he continues to be Chairman.

My earliest impression of him was that he had a quality of Christian, or more precisely prophetic, courage. It is therefore perhaps no coincidence that his subsequent career propelled him into prominence as a Church leader due to his clear insight into the relevance of the Christian Gospel to the daily socio-political realities in which we all live, and his extraordinary capacity for faith and steadfastness.

In Season and out of Season, is subtitled *Sermons to a Nation*. However, it could equally be subtitled *Sermons to the Church*. For David Gitari is not a self-righteous castigator of secular political leaders and their machineries of control. Rather, he is pre-eminently a preacher and teacher of the Word of God. The setting and background of each sermon given provides a vivid picture of the context and realities in which the Bishop carries out his ministry.

In 1988, Uzima Press in Nairobi, Kenya, published *Let the Bishop speak*. This was based on expository sermons he had preached in the four Sundays in the month of June 1987, and which had generated much interest as well as controversy in the country. Reflecting on those sermons and the comments they attracted, Bishop Gitari then wrote:

> Every trained preacher knows that there are many styles or methods of preaching. I am however attracted to what is known as expository preaching. . . . Expository preaching embraces both preaching and teaching. It includes sharing an understanding of the historical and spiritual context in which different Bible passages are set. Furthermore, the expository preacher would fail in his duty if he did not let the message of the Bible come alive to the modern hearer. Though written thousands of years ago, the Word of God is meant to be effective in our lives today and it is the task of the preacher to make his hearers realise this fact. This process of bringing God's word to bear on our contemporary world is part of what is meant by a prophetic ministry.

This book gives us an even wider range of David Gitari's prophetic preaching and shows him to be a truly 'trained preacher'.

It also illustrates one of the distinctive features of current African Christian scholarship and witness, namely, its holistic, practical and mission-oriented nature. The majority of Africa's Christian theologians are not ivory-tower academics, irrelevant to the daily struggles of the ordinary Christian. They are practical theologians and active Church-men and women, seeking from the Gospel answers to burning issues.

Regnum Books (Africa), the publishing arm of the African Theological Fellowship, is particularly pleased that *In Season and out of Season*, the work of its own distinguished Chairman, should be its maiden publication. We commend it warmly to all who seek an insight into the nature of Christian witness in Africa today. All who read it will discover also its relevance to Christian ministry and witness elsewhere in the world.

Akropong-Akuapem, Ghana
January 1996

Kwame Bediako
Chairman, INFEMIT
General Secretary, ATF

Biographical Notes

Born on 16th September 1937 to Evangelist Samuel Mukuba and Jessie Njuku in Ngiriambu, Kirinyaga, David Gitari preached his first sermon at the age of fifteen to his home congregation of Ngiriambu.

He studied at Kangaru High School from 1955–1958 and joined Nairobi University in 1959 where he graduated in 1964 with B.A. honours, and during which time he was greatly involved in mission to schools and universities in Africa. From 1968–1971 he studied Theology at Bristol as an external student of the University of London and graduated with a B.D. From 1972–1975 he served as General Secretary of the Bible Society of Kenya, and Chairman of Kenya Students Christian Fellowship (KSCF). He was awarded an honorary D.D. by Ashley Seminary, Ohio, U.S.A. in 1983.

He was Bishop of the Diocese of Mt. Kenya East from 1975 to 1990. Currently the Bishop of Kirinyaga Diocese, Bishop Gitari is also the Dean of the Church of the Province of Kenya.

During his ministry as Bishop, he has powerfully and fearlessly used the pulpit to prophesy to the nation, thus helping to change the course of political affairs in both his district of Kirinyaga and the nation as a whole.

This book, a collection of sermons preached since 1975, is evident of his prophetic ministry. Bishop Gitari has travelled widely and his ecumenical involvement has put him on several committees, local, national and international. He has served as a member of the Strategy Committee of the Lausanne Congress on World Evangelisation; the Chairman of the World Evangelical Fellowship Theological Commission; Vice President of the World Council of Churches Commission on World Mission and Evangelism; member of the Anglican-Roman Catholic International Commission (ARCIC); member of the International Anglican Liturgical Commission.

He is currently Chairman of the African Theological Fellowship; Chairman of C.A.P.A. Liturgical Commission; member of the International Fellowship of Evangelical Mission Theologians (INFEMIT); Chairman of the London based 'Christians relating to Muslims' project. In Kenya he has been for many years the chairman of the Provincial Board of Theological Education and Liturgy and has greatly spear-headed liturgical renewal efforts in the Church of the Province of Kenya.

Preface

On many occasions at the end of a Church service I have been asked whether I have copies of my sermon. This has led me to prepare written texts of my sermons which would later be duplicated and sold by our department of communications.

When Patrick Benson was appointed the Publications Secretary in the Diocese of Mt Kenya East in 1986, he made it a priority to gather together all the prophetic sermons I had preached since the assassination of a renowned legislator, Josiah Mwangi Kariuki, in March 1975. Benson put together and edited many of the sermons. But the manuscript was stolen in Nairobi as he was delivering it to Uzima Press for publication. Benson, formerly a tutor at the then St Andrew's Institute for Mission and Evangelism, Kabare, returned to the UK before he had completed the task. I wish to thank him very much for the work he did in preparing, editing and typing the early sermons.

His successor was the Rev Joyce Karuri who during the last half of 1994 worked very hard at typesetting and editing the manuscript. At one time, owing to repeated power failures, she lost all the work she had put in the computer for several weeks but had the courage to do it all over again. This sounds very much like the prophet Jeremiah who had to re-write a scroll destroyed and burnt by King Jehoiakim who found the message too devastating to bear. However, the culprit this time was the Kenya Power and Lighting Company.

Rev Dr Chris Sugden, the Director of the Oxford Centre for Mission Studies, during a short visit to Nairobi, read the final draft and made useful comments and corrections. I am most grateful to him.

In preparing these sermons I was greatly influenced by the readable New Testament commentaries of Dr William Barclay. The works of Rev Dr John W R Stott have also greatly influenced my understanding and practice of expository preaching. In this respect I have normally expounded a passage of scripture and applied it to the contemporary situation and circumstances. I must also pay tribute to Martin Luther King Jr whose expository sermons contained in his book *Strength to Love* influenced me greatly.

I attended the Lausanne Congress on World Evangelization in 1974, one year before I was consecrated bishop. At Lausanne the Evangelicals confessed to having put a wedge between evangelism and social-political activities. Since that time my understanding of Church-state relationship has been greatly influenced by members of the International Fellowship of Evangelical Mission Theologians (INFEMIT) and especially Rene Padilla of

Argentina, Vinay Samuel of India, Ron Sider of the USA and Canada, Kwame Bediako of Ghana, Chris Sugden of Britain, Peter Kuzmic of Croatia and the late David J Bosch of South Africa.

I am most grateful to Faith Ndirangu and Abishag Kairu – former secretaries in the department of communications – for helping in the typing of the sermons. I am also grateful to Bilha Koigi, my personal secretary, who has kept records of some of the sermons.

To all these and many others who have contributed in one way or another, I am sincerely grateful.

The Rt. Rev. Dr. David M. Gitari
Bishop of Kirinyaga

1

May We Dwell in Unity

THE SETTING

On 3rd March 1975 the Kenyan nation was stunned to hear of the murder of Josiah Mwangi Kariuki, a hero of the resistance against the colonial government and populist Member of Parliament from Nyandarua. J.M, as he was popularly known, is said to have been picked up by a party of unidentified men and driven to the Ngong Hills, where a shepherd boy discovered his mutilated body a few days later. A period of nationwide unrest followed; university students took to the city streets, demanding to be told the names of those who killed J.M. A number of bombs were set off in public places and anonymous pamphlets implicated the government in the killing.

An inquiry was instituted into the circumstances of J.M's assassination. It met with considerable obstruction and, although nobody was ever charged, speculation was rife that some top government figures were involved. So the National Christian Council of Kenya (NCCK), concerned about the political situation that threatened the stability of the country, declared a week of national repentance and prayer. The Rev David M Gitari was then General Secretary of the Bible Society of Kenya (a few months away from becoming the first Bishop of the Diocese of Mt Kenya East). He had no pulpit of his own, yet he was often invited to preach at various Churches. NCCK asked him to speak on the Voice of Kenya's 'Lift Up Your Hearts' programme which came every day (except Sundays) for 5 minutes just before the 7am news bulletin. He called his talks 'Lift up the Nation'. On Sunday, 20th April 1975 he preached this sermon which was broadcast live from Nairobi Baptist Church. Included also are excerpts of the daily talks on 'Lift Up the Nation'.

THE SERMON

1. A Holy Church in a Holy Nation

Christians throughout Kenya are observing this day as a Sunday of repentance and prayer. Indeed since last Monday special prayers have been offered for our nation by Christians throughout Kenya. This has been first and foremost a week for those of us who are Christians to repent of our failure to give a lead to the nation in the struggle for justice, unity and liberty. Disunity among members of the Church of Christ has made it difficult to speak with one voice, and as a result the Church has neglected its purpose to be the salt of the earth and the light of the world. This week of repentance and prayer therefore has the object of drawing Christians to the unity whose basis is truth in the fulfillment of our Lord's prayer: 'May they be one, so that the world will believe that you sent me' (Jn. 17:21). We Christians are to blame in that we have not courageously and with one voice declared the righteousness which God demands of a nation set apart to serve him. Kenya quite rightly claims to be a 'glorious nation'; that is precisely the translation of the Kiswahili words *Taifa Tukufu*. Such glory in a nation should denote majesty and perfection, especially in righteousness. This glory should be found in a nation called to be holy.

In Old Testament days Israel was a nation set apart to serve God. In adopting the word 'glory' for our nation, we accept a calling to which we must live up. We are consecrated and set apart to render true and glorious service to God and humanity. It is the Church's heavy responsibility to remind a nation, called to be holy, of the standard of righteousness and justice which alone can exalt that nation. The Christian community must be an ever present reminder to the state that it exists only as a servant of God and human beings. To be able to fulfil this task, Christian leaders throughout Kenya must come out of their ecclesiastical ghettos and ivory towers to lead the citizens of this country in giving active practical moral support to the state when it upholds the standards of righteousness which God expects from a glorious nation. When our nation upholds those standards of righteousness, our support for the authorities will be 100%. If, however, those in authority depart from the righteousness which God expects of a nation, the Church should follow the footsteps of the prophets and the apostles in declaring boldly the righteousness and judgement of God.

However, it is impossible and hypocritical of the members of the Church of Christ to try to fulfil this task unless the Christian community is living at a different standard from the rest of society, unless it enjoys a distinct and more honest fellowship, and has an extraordinary unselfishness and supernatural love in its activities. It is ridiculous to challenge other people about tribalism, nepotism and disunity if the same characteristics are the order of the day in the Church itself. 'If the salt has lost its taste, it is no longer good for anything except to be thrown out and be trodden under foot by men' [Mt. 5:13].

May the call for repentance reach every Christian man and woman in this land, so that we can truly become the salt of the earth and the light of the world. St Peter reminds Christians that 'You are a chosen race, a royal priesthood, a holy nation, God's own people that you may declare the wonderful deeds of him who brought you out of darkness into his marvellous light' (1 Pet. 2:9). To guide Christians in their prayers the National Christian Council of Kenya (NCCK) has asked the Churches to make the first stanza of the national anthem the basis of our prayers this week. It runs thus: 'O God of all Creation, Bless this our land and nation, Justice be our shield and defender, May we dwell in unity, peace and liberty , Plenty be found within our borders'.

A national anthem is a hymn or song expressing the patriotic sentiments of a people. It is the Magna Carta of a people's personal and political freedom. Often when the music of the National Anthem is played, it captures my emotions so much that I am not ashamed to stand to attention and concentrate wholly on the patriotic sentiments that it embodies. What are these patriotic sentiments? They include the desire for blessing, justice, unity, peace, liberty and plenty to be bestowed on our nation. This is not mere sentimentalism. Rather, it is a prayer to God, the creator of all, to send his blessings on our nation.

2. Bless this Our Land and Nation

Thus begins our National Anthem. Yet it should be noted that God does not bless his people unconditionally. As the Psalmist says: 'Blessed are all who fear the Lord, who walk in his ways' (Ps. 128:1). And again, 'Blessed are the people whose Lord is God' (Ps. 144:15b). It is the people who fear God and whose God is the Lord who are blessed. In the opening words of his Sermon on the Mount, our Lord Jesus Christ summarized the characteristics of the people who are given God's blessings. They are the poor in spirit, those who mourn, those who hunger and thirst for righteousness, the merciful, the pure in heart, the peacemakers and those who are persecuted because of their righteousness.

When we ask God to bless us, we Kenyans must in turn be God-fearing. But we cannot describe this nation as God-fearing, when we create an atmosphere that makes it so easy for the demonic powers of this world to take the upper hand; when an individual or a group of people can with much ease plant the bomb outside the East African Railway Station which exploded on 1st March 1975, killing 27 innocent lives. By our relative silence when Gama Pinto and Thomas Joseph Mboya were mercilessly gunned down and removed from our presence, we made it easier for the wicked to strike again. And so on 3rd March 1975, the nation was informed that the Hon. Josiah Mwangi Kariuki was dead! Yet those in authority have not kept their word, that they would not leave any stone unturned till they arrested the killers of J.M. Our failure to hunger and thirst for righteousness means that our prayers for God to bless us may go unanswered. Instead of blessings, our nation could be cursed for the wanton act of shedding the blood of innocent people for mere purposes of self preservation.

We are grateful that parliament has appointed a special select committee to investigate the murder of J.M. It is our prayer that God will overrule the possible obstacles which would otherwise hinder the committee from doing its work to a satisfactory end, and that they would wisely and courageously seek and find the truth. The nation has a great expectation that the J.M Probe Committee will come up with the truth, the truth which we hope will bring to an end all the destructive bickering and rumour mongering.

3. Justice be our Shield and Defender

God's blessings cannot come in a vacuum. Our Lord Jesus Christ said: 'Blessed are they who hunger and thirst for righteousness, for they shall be satisfied' [Mt. 5:6]. By this Jesus meant that we must have an intense thirst for justice and righteousness in the world. This is not mere abstract longing; it is an intense and specific hunger and thirst for total justice in every aspect of our national life. The Book of Proverbs gives us a number of insights as to why we should hunger and thirst for the righteousness of our nation. It is because:

Righteousness makes a nation great;
Sin is a disgrace to the nation.
Kings cannot tolerate evil, because
Justice is what makes a government strong.

The NCCK has requested the Churches to pray for justice in different aspects of our national life, including the business and commercial world. Businessmen should be moved by the patriotic sentiments of our national anthem and should refrain from temptations to make quick money by smuggling maize, rice, sugar and charcoal; and from hoarding essential commodities. Justice means that at such a time of inflation, *wananchi* (citizens) should be spared from unfair sales practices and exorbitant prices.

Smugglers are now doing their business with a 'sense of humour', as one newspaper puts it: we hear and read of sugar being exported as 'barley' and 'soda ash'. Maize goes out as 'unfit for human consumption', while rice is labelled 'Danger: Petrol'. Charcoal is still posing as charcoal but illegally leaving the port. The judgement of God will come upon all smugglers, for in the Book of Proverbs we read: 'If you try to make a profit dishonestly, you will get your family into trouble. Don't take bribes, and you will live longer' [Prov. 15:27].

Likewise those who are engaging themselves in unholy activities such as planting bombs in this holy nation should heed these words: 'Those who plan evil are in for a rude surprise, but those who work for good will find happiness' [Prov. 12:20]. Let us pray that justice will shield and defend J.M. Kariuki whose innocent blood has been shed.

4. Peace

Our Lord Jesus Christ said, 'Blessed are the peacemakers for they shall be called the children of God' [Mt. 5:9]. Peace in our national life is another patriotic sentiment of our national anthem. We should not only pray for peace. Rather we should also struggle to bring about 'peace on earth and goodwill towards men'.

Peacemakers who are promised a blessing are not necessarily peace lovers; as Dr William Barclay says, 'If a man loves peace in the wrong way he succeeds in making trouble and not peace'. We may, for instance, allow a threatening and dangerous situation to develop, our defence being that 'for the sake of peace we shouldn't take any action'. Many people think that by refusing to face a situation, they are working for peace. But this only serves to bring about an *illusion* of peace and mere postponement of trouble. The peace referred to does not come from the *evasion* of issues; it comes from *facing* them and dealing with them. What this beatitude demands is not the passive acceptance of things because we are afraid of trouble, but rather working to establish peace.

Since our God is not a God of chaos but of peace, he is the one who gives permission for governing authorities to exist. To avoid anarchy and chaos, God has given authority to our government to rule over us. It is the duty of every citizen to obey the state authorities, and the latter have the duty to give protection and security to every human being living within the boundaries of a nation. As St Paul says, when the authorities are fulfilling their duty they are working for God, therefore we should pay taxes and show respect and honour [Rom. 13:4–5]. In giving security to every person, those in authority are serving God. We have a duty to pray earnestly for all those in authority that they may be agents of true peace and may be enabled to bring to justice the murderers and bomb planters. Our prayer however is not that sinners may die but rather that they may repent and find forgiveness in God. In his first letter to Timothy, Paul gives some instructions regarding a Christian's duty to pray: 'First of all, then, I urge that petitions and prayers, requests and thanksgivings be offered to God for all people, for kings and all others who are in authority, that we may live a quiet and peaceful life, in entire godliness and proper conduct' (1Tim. 2:1–3).

5. Unity

For a nation to be strong, unity is essential. We should however distinguish between deceptive unity and true unity; between a false, and a true spirit of *harambee*. The basis of true unity is love and truth.

Love, the basis of unity

A husband and wife are called one flesh because they are united in love. If there is no love their marriage becomes very shaky and unstable, because love has grown cold. The biblical teaching about a human being is not that he or she is a collection of chemical elements or like other creatures. Rather the Bible portrays humanity as 'made in the image of God'. It is for that reason that our fellow-human beings are to be loved and served and not exploited or eliminated. It is because we are capable of loving God that we should love those who are made in his image. This is indeed the true basis of all democracy. If we love God, then that love will overflow into the lives of others. Love means the refusal to see, think of or deal with your neighbours except in the light of what Christ has done for them as individuals, supremely giving his life for them. In a nation where men and women give their total love to God, this perception directs their thoughts and love and becomes the dynamic of their actions; consequently all barriers to unity will be removed; whether it be racism, tribalism, enmity or jealousy. Such love can be found only in Jesus Christ, who loved us so much that he gave his life for us.

Truth, the basis of unity

Unity that is not founded on truth is no unity at all. One of the things marring our national unity is rumour-mongering. Rumour 'is general talk of doubtful accuracy'. All people of goodwill should refrain from spreading such talk. We have a responsibility for checking our facts before we pass on any doubtful information.

However, in the light of human nature, it is unrealistic to expect people not to engage in rumour-mongering if at the same time the truth is not revealed and defended. Human beings have a great propensity to engage their minds in speculation, especially where no information is given on a subject of public interest. Responsible citizens will however avoid the temptation to spread 'general talk of doubtful accuracy'. We condemn vehemently the cowardly circulation of anonymous and malicious pamphlets. Those anonymous pamphleteers should come out in the open and substantiate their allegations.

An appeal for national unity must be an appeal that we may be united in truth, but not in falsehood. It is quite possible for a tribe or a group of people to unite by entering into a secret superstitious oath. That kind of unity is founded on fear, not on truth. The superstitious fear is that breaking such an oath would bring disaster to an individual. But once a person is set free from the bondage of superstition, he is freed from secret tribal oaths. Our Lord Jesus says: 'If you continue in my word you will know the truth and the truth will set you free' (Jn. 8: 31). The unity which is founded on truth is permanent whereas unity that is based on falsehood is only temporary, and is characterized by fear and superficial peace. This is one of the greatest lessons we can learn from the Watergate scandal. Top government officials entered into a deceptive unity so as to acquire power by wrong methods. When the scandal was discovered they again united to cover it up. But because this unity was not based on truth, their inner peace disappeared and they continued with their troubled administration until their sin found them out.

6. Freedom

Liberty, otherwise referred to as freedom, is yet another word that expresses our patriotic sentiments. The biblical concept of freedom does not set us free to do whatever we want, but rather to do what we ought to do. Imagine a fish in a pond. It is entirely free as long as it swims within the bounds of the pond. If one day it decided to seek freedom from the restrictions of the pond and jumped out onto the dry land, it would lose all its freedom because it is meant to enjoy life within the environment of the water. Similarly for a person to enjoy true freedom, he must swim within the environment which God created for him. That environment is love. We must swim in the sea of love if we want to find true liberty for our hearts and for our nation. If people were swimming in the sea of love there would be no bomb explosions and no secret plots of any kind. Jesus said, 'Every one who commits sin is a slave to sin . . . So if the Son makes you free, you will be free indeed' (Jn. 8:36).

7. The Right to Life

On 10th December 1948, the United Nations General Assembly proclaimed the Universal Declaration of Human Rights. The Declaration includes the following human rights:

The right to life,
The right to liberty and security,
The right to education,
Equality before the law,
Freedom of movement and religion,
Freedom of Association and,
Freedom to marry and have a family.

It is no surprise that this historic declaration of human rights begins by asserting that a person has the right to life. The Covenant of Lausanne

Congress on World Evangelization (LCWE) held at Lausanne, Switzerland in July 1974 states:

> Mankind is made in the image of God and as a result every person regardless of race, religion, colour, culture, class, sex, age, has an intrinsic dignity and for this reason he should be respected and served and not exploited or eliminated.

You are created in the image of God and for that reason nobody should deny you the right to exist. The Bible presents physical life as the creation of God who alone is the source of life, and human beings have no independent right to shed blood and take life. A person does not even have the liberty to take his own life. He is accountable to God for what he has done to himself or his fellow human being. When Cain murdered his brother Abel, God asked him, 'Where is Abel your brother'? And Cain answered: 'I do not know. Am I my brother's keeper'? And God said to Cain, 'What have you done Cain? The voice of your brother's blood is crying to me from the ground and now you are cursed . . .'. Today God is asking Kenyans, 'Where is your brother J.M. Kariuki?' And those who assassinated him or planned his assassination are saying, 'Am I my brother's keeper?'

The story of Cain shows clearly that a person's blood, after his death, may have profound effects, not through the persistent activity of life released, but because of the significance of the life taken. Unlike other creatures, a human being is unique because he is made in the image of God. For this reason it is a terrible sin for anyone to trifle with human life. Because he is created in the image of God, a human being has an intrinsic dignity and for this reason his life should be respected, not eliminated. And where a human being in any country has allegedly committed a crime deserving the death penalty, he must be given the opportunity to defend himself.

The cries of a person whose blood is shed without fair trial reaches the heavenly seat of God who in return pronounces a curse and not a blessing. Even in our African tradition, shedding the blood of an innocent person defiles the land and there is need of cleansing the whole clan or tribe where the crime was committed.

Are you your brother's keeper? Yes indeed you are. And for that reason you should refrain from any deliberate activity which could jeopardize the life of your neighbour today and always.

8. Plenty be found Within our Borders

For the nation to receive the blessings of plenty, certain conditions must be met:

a) As we live in a fallen world, people must till the land and exploit natural resources. In other words, to be blessed with plenty, people must work hard.
b) Everyone in the nation should be given the opportunity to promote their own well-being. As the Universal Declaration of Human Rights says, a human being has the right to work under favourable conditions with equal pay for equal work.
c) When God created Adam and Eve he said to them, 'Be fruitful and

multiply, fill the earth and subdue it and have dominion over the fish of the sea and over the birds of the air and over every living thing that moves on the earth' [Gen. 1:28]. Here lies humanity's warrant to exploit natural resources responsibly. However he has no warrant, at the same time, to exploit his fellow human beings for his own benefit.

d) A nation cannot be said to be enjoying the blessings of plenty if wealth is concentrated in the hands of a few people. The Old Testament prophets condemned vehemently the property grabbers of their day. About 700 years before Christ, the prophet Micah said these words: 'How terrible it will be for those who lie in bed and plan evil! When morning comes, as soon as they have a chance, they do the evil they planned. When they want fields, they take them, when they want houses, they take them. No man's family or property is safe'. And so the Lord says, "I am planning to bring disaster on you, and you will not be able to escape it. You are going to find yourselves in trouble and then you will not walk so proudly any more. When that time comes people will use your story as an example of disaster . . ." [Mic. 2:1–4]. For a nation to enjoy the blessing of plenty there should be:

   i) Justice which involves the establishment of equal rights for all.
   ii) Unity which removes all barriers to a true spirit of *harambee*. Such unity must have the basis of love and truth.
   iii) Peace which creates the right conditions for enabling man to make full use of his talents.
   iv) Liberty which grants a person their basic human rights to enable them to render true service to God and other people.

And this is why we sing: 'O God of all Creation, . . .'

THE AFTERMATH OF THE TALKS AND THE SERMON

After I had given the fourth 'Lift up the nation' talk on Thursday, I received a telephone call from the Voice of Kenya inviting me for a dialogue. I went to V.O.K at 3pm and I was ushered into a room where I found seven top officials from the Ministry of Information waiting for me. I greeted them but none responded except Rev Gichuhi who was then Director of Religious Programmes. The Chairman, Mr Kangwana, informed me that my radio talks were very disturbing as they seemed to imply that the government was involved in the murder of Mr J.M. Kariuki. But I informed the meeting that if my talks were disturbing then they had achieved their purpose, as the gospel is very disturbing to sinners. I further reiterated that every human being is made in the image of God and has an intrinsic dignity. Because of this he should be respected and served and not exploited or eliminated. Pointing at each of them, I emphasized: 'You are created in the image of God and no one has the right to destroy God's image in you'. The chairman replied: 'If that is what you are saying, then continue'. The remaining two talks were not censured and the following Sunday I preached at a live broadcast service from the Nairobi Baptist Church summarizing the six talks in my sermon.

The next day, Rev Gichuhi telephoned to say that the manuscript of the sermon was needed at the State House, Mombasa where President Kenyatta was on a working holiday. My secretary started typing the manuscript at 4pm while the Rev Gichuhi waited for it so impatiently that it could not even be proofread. It was then sent by Express Mail to Mombasa. For the next two weeks we waited anxiously to hear the verdict from Mombasa. But finding myself unable to concentrate on my work in Nairobi, I took a holiday and went to my home village in Kirinyaga, not only to wait for the verdict, but also to pray over a request by the Christians of the newly created Diocese of Mt Kenya East that I become their Bishop. The Electoral College had unanimously elected me the previous week but I had expressed the need to be allowed more time to pray.

Two weeks later I received a telephone call from the Permanent Secretary in the Office of the President, who wanted to see me. Assuming that this concerned the sermon, I called all the members of staff at the Bible House for special prayers as I went to face the wrath of the authorities.

Carrying a copy of the sermon I walked into the building where I expected to find a good number of top civil servants. But when I was ushered in I found only the Permanent Secretary, Geoffrey Kariithi, who received me warmly and took me by surprise with the question, 'Why are you delaying in accepting your appointment as Bishop of Mt Kenya East'? He then took out his diary, and with my consent rang the Archbishop, and we fixed 20th July 1975 as the date of my consecration and enthronement.

2

Shattered Dreams

Romans 15:20

Sermon preached to the students of Kenyatta University College in November 1978 during a Mission to the University Students.

THE SERMON

> My ambition has always been to proclaim the Good News in places where Christ has not been heard of, so as not to build on a foundation laid by someone else. . . . But now that I have finished my work in these regions, and since I have been waiting for so many years to come and see you, I hope to do so now. I would like to see you on my way to Spain, and be helped by you to go there, after I have enjoyed visiting you for a while [Rom. 15:20, 23–24].

One of the most agonizing problems within our human experience is that few if any of us live to see our fondest hopes fulfilled. The dreams of our childhood, the expectations of our future years are seen to be like unfinished symphonies. Is there any one of us who has not faced the agony of blasted hopes and shattered dreams?

In Paul's letter to the Roman Christians we find a good illustration of this vexing problem of disappointed hopes. Paul's ruling passion was to preach the Good News where Christ had not been heard of. His ambition was to enter new frontiers. And so, having preached in Asia Minor and Greece, his purpose was to go on to Spain. He did not want to go to Rome as a missionary because other apostles had already been there. His dream was to go to Spain, but via Rome in order to salute the Christians there.

We are given two reasons for Paul's great ambition to go to Spain. Firstly, Spain was at the very western end of Europe. It was, in a sense, the limit of the known world. And, as Jesus had commanded his disciples to preach the gospel in Jerusalem, Judea, Samaria and the uttermost parts of the earth, Paul may have felt that by going to Spain he was fulfilling the Lord's command. Paul would characteristically wish to take the Good News of Jesus so far that there was no farther to go.

Secondly, Spain was at this time experiencing a kind of blaze of genius.

Many of the greatest men in the Roman Empire were Spaniards. These included Lucan the epic poet, Martial the master of epigram, Quintilian the greatest teacher of oratory in his day, and Seneca, the great stoic philosopher, who later became the chief minister of Nero the Roman Emperor.

It may well be that Paul was saying to himself, 'If only I can get to Spain, I might possibly be able to touch the hearts of some of these great thinkers who would in turn use their intellect and talents to win the empire for Jesus Christ.' If that was the case, his ambition was good.

The Church does not require only simple minds. There is need for philosophers, lawyers, doctors, teachers and scientists to be part and parcel of the Church of Christ. But we know that Paul never fulfilled his dream to reach Spain. He went to Jerusalem, and because of his daring faith in Jesus Christ he was taken a prisoner, and for two years he was detained at Caesarea-by-the-sea, during which time his case was heard by the governors Felix and Festus and by King Agrippa. He then appealed to appear before Caesar himself. A shipwreck occurred on the journey to Rome but Paul reached the city only to be confined to a cell for about two years. He seems to have died in Rome at the hands of Emperor Nero in about 64 A.D. Paul died without his dream of reaching Spain being fulfilled.

Our lives mirror many similar experiences. Who has not set out towards some distant 'Spain', some momentous goal or some glorious realization, only to learn at last that they must settle for much less? Instead of walking a free person in the streets of Rome you find yourself in a cell and thus you never reach the Spain of your dreams. In other words, our reach always exceeds our grasp.

After leading the Children of Israel out of their Egyptian bondage, Moses could only watch the land of Canaan as a distant Spain. He never stepped onto the land of Promise.

Paul kept on praying fervently that the thorn might be removed from his flesh, but the pain and irritation continued to the end of his days.

Henry Martyn, the young genius from Cambridge University, fell in love with Lydia just before he left England to start a missionary career in India in 1805. From then on, Lydia became his heart's deepest desire. But he died in Persia in 1812 on his way back to England to marry her.

After struggling for years to achieve independence, Mahatma Gandhi witnessed a bloody war between Hindus and Muslims, and the subsequent division of India and Pakistan shattered his heart's desire for a united India.

After leading the Civil Rights movement in America for a decade, Martin Luther King Jr. did not live to enjoy the fruits of his labour but fell to an assassin's bullet.

Bitterness and Resentment

Before we determine how to live in a world where our highest hopes are not satisfied, we must ask what one does under such circumstances. There are many people whose first reaction to such frustrations is to develop a core of bitterness and resentment. The person who pursues this path is likely to develop a callous or hardened attitude – a cold heart and a bitter hatred towards God, towards those with whom he lives, and towards himself. Since he cannot come to terms with the reality of life, he becomes hostile towards other people. He may be extremely cruel to people close to him. Meanness becomes his dominating characteristic. He loves no one and requires love from no one. He trusts no one and does not expect others to trust him. He finds faults with everything and everybody and continually complains. He is like Macbeth soliloquizing that: 'life is but a walking shadow, a poor player, that struts and frets his hour upon the stage, and then is heard no more. It is a tale told by an idiot, full of sound and fury, signifying nothing'.

Such an attitude poisons the soul and scars the personality; always harming the person himself more than anyone else. Medical science reveals that such physical ailments as arthritis and gastric ulcers have on occasions been encouraged by bitter resentments. Psychosomatic medicine deals with the bodily sickness which comes from mental illness and shows how deep resentment may result in physical deterioration.

Complete Withdrawal

Another common reaction by those who have failed to reach the distant 'Spain' of their dreams is that they withdraw into themselves and eventually become complete introverts. Such people lose their zest for living and attempt to escape by lifting their minds to a realm of cold indifference. 'Detachment' is the word that best describes them.

> They are 'too unconcerned to love and too passionless to hate; too detached to be selfish and too lifeless to be unselfish; too indifferent to experience joy and too cold to experience sorrow. They are neither dead nor alive, they merely exist'.
>
> Their eyes do not see the beauty of nature; their ears are too insensitive to majestic sounds of great music, and their hands do not respond to the touch of a charming little baby. Nothing of the aliveness of life is left in them; only the dull motion of bare existence. Disappointed hopes lead them to extreme cynicism. This reaction is based on an attempt to escape from life. Psychiatrists say that when an individual attempts to escape from reality, his personality becomes thinner and thinner until it finally splits.
>
> (Martin Luther King Jr., *Strength to Love*)

Fatalistic Philosophy

A third way by which people respond to disappointments of a distant 'Spain' is to adopt a fatalistic philosophy which teaches that whatever happens must happen and that all events are determined by necessity.

As Martin Luther King further says, 'Fatalism implies that everything is foreordained and inescapable. People who subscribe to this philosophy succumb to an absolute resignation to that which they consider to be their fate and think of themselves as little more than little orphans cast into terrifying immensities of space. Because they believe that man has no freedom, they seek neither to deliberate or make decisions; they'd rather wait passively for external forces to decide for them. They never actively seek to change their circumstances for they believe all circumstances are controlled by irresistible and foreordained forces. Indeed some fatalists are religious people who think of God as the determiner and controller of destiny. Believing that freedom is a myth, fatalists surrender to paralyzing determination which concludes that:

The moving finger writes, and having writ
Moves on; nor all our piety or wit
Shall lure it back to cancel half a line,
Nor all your tears wash out a word of it.
(Fitzgerald, *The Rubaiyat of Omar Khayham*)

To sink into this fatalistic attitude is both intellectually and psychologically stifling. Freedom is part of the essence of man. Hence, by denying himself freedom, the fatalist becomes a puppet, not a person. He is right in his conviction that there is no absolute freedom, and that freedom always operates within the context of pre-ordained structure. Freedom is always within the context of destiny. You are free to walk from Jerusalem to Jericho. But before you start your journey, remember that there are robbers on that road, and you might be attacked. But you *are* free! Freedom is the act of deliberating, deciding and responding within our destined nature. Even if destiny may prevent us from going to some attractive 'Spain', we do have the capacity to accept such disappointment, to respond to it and to do something about disappointment itself. Fatalism makes an individual helplessly inadequate for life.'

Fatalism is also based on an appalling concept of God; for everything, good or evil, is considered to represent the will of God. A healthy faith rises above the idea that God wills evil. Although he may permit evil in order to preserve freedom of choice, God does not *cause* evil.

The Answer

The answer lies in our willing acceptance of unwilled and unfortunate circumstances even as we cling still to our radiant hope, our acceptance of finite disappointment even as we adhere to infinite hope. This is not the grim, bitter acceptance of fatalism but the triumphant achievement of facing life as it is. You must face your shattered dreams honestly. To follow the escapist method of attempting to put the disappointment out of your mind leads only to psychologically furious repression. Place your failure at the forefront of your mind and stare daringly at it. Ask yourself, 'How can I transform this liability into an asset'? Inside the Roman jail, Paul may have asked: 'How can I, confined in this small cell and unable to reach Spain, change this dungeon of shame into a haven of redemptive suffering'?

Almost everything that happens to us can be turned into a source of blessing. It humbles us, breaks our self centred pride, and helps us to sympathize with others.

Many of the world's most influential personalities have exchanged their thorns in the flesh for crowns of glory. Charles Darwin suffered from recurrent physical illness. Robert Louis Stevenson was plagued with tuberculosis. Hellen Keller was blind and deaf. Loyola, the founder of the Jesuit movement, was a cripple. The Emperor Napoleon was epileptic.

Handel wrote the famous 'Hallelujah Chorus' when his health and fortune had reached their lowest ebb, when his left side was paralyzed, and when his creditors had seized him and threatened him with imprisonment. The 'Hallelujah Chorus' was born, not in a holiday villa in 'Spain', but in a narrow and undesirable 'Roman cell'.

St Paul is described as a short bow-legged man with small eyes and a persistent physical ailment, 'a thorn in the flesh'. And Timothy, Paul's son in the faith, is said to have been a young timid lad with a weak stomach.

How familiar is the experience of longing for 'Spain' and having to settle for a Roman prison! How much less familiar is the transforming of the shattered remains of disappointed expectations into opportunities to serve God's purposes! Powerful living involves such victories over one's soul and situation.

The world is full of storms. Like the storms on the sea of Galilee, the storms of life are to be faced with courage. This is the kind of courage that Paul possessed, the courage to be. His life was a continual round of disappointment. On every side were broken plans and shattered dreams. Planning to go to Spain, he was confined in a Roman cell; hoping to go to Bithynia, he was sidetracked to Troas and Macedonia. His missionary activities were full of frustrations.

In everything we do, we show that we are God's servants by enduring troubles and difficulties with patience. But as servants of God we commend ourselves in every way through great endurance in afflictions; hardships and calamities; beatings and imprisonment; tumults and labours; watchings and hunger. Paul's gallant mission for Christ was measured 'in journeys often, in perils of water, perils of robbers, perils of my own countrymen, in perils with health, perils in the city, perils in the wilderness, on sea and among false brethren' (2 Cor. 11:26).

Paul faced all these troubles courageously. He says: 'I have learned in whatever circumstances I am, therewith to be content' (Philp. 4:11b). He had learned to stand tall and without despairing amidst the disappointments of life.

Turning a Liability into an Asset: Paul's method

> I want you to know my brothers that the things that have happened to me have really helped to advance the gospel as a result. The whole palace guard and all the others here know that I am a servant of Christ. And my being in prison has given most of the brothers more confidence in the Lord, so that they grow bolder all the time in preaching the message without fear [Philp. 2:12–14].

When Paul found himself in a prison cell in Rome instead of being in Spain, he did not spend time in regrets. Instead he took what appeared to be a liability and turned it into an asset for the glory of God. Writing to his friends in Philippi he tells them that, 'the things that have happened to me have really helped to advance the gospel' (Philp. 1:12).

While in his prison confinement Paul did three things to advance the gospel:

1. He encouraged the brethren who used to visit him in prison. They were going there to sympathize with him but instead it was Paul the prisoner who took control of the situation and urged the Christians to stand firm and to proclaim the gospel courageously and without fear. As a result, they went back full of confidence and in turn encouraged other believers. Hence, writing to the Philippians, Paul had good reason to say, 'My being in prison has given most of the brothers more confidence in the Lord – so they grow bolder all the time in preaching the message without fear' [Philp. 1:4].

It was a very difficult time for Christians in Rome as the Emperor Nero had become very suspicious of believers. At first the Roman authorities tolerated Christianity as they assumed it was the same as Judaism which was *religio licita* (a permitted religion). However, the authorities started to notice that Christianity and Judaism were very different, and persecution of Christians began. Nero himself had set on fire some parts of the great city of Rome, and then blamed it on the Christians. The signs were clear that a great persecution against Christians was in the making. And Paul in his Roman cell lost no opportunity in offering the brethren what they needed most: courage and strength to face the worst!

2. Paul also took the opportunity to evangelize even his captors, including all the soldiers who took turns to guard him. The Praetorian Guard were the imperial Guards of Rome. They were a body of ten thousand picked troops, soldiers who had excelled in many battles and who for twelve years served as the Emperor's private bodyguard. When the Emperor died it was they who chose his successor.

When Paul arrived in Rome he was allowed to look for private lodging but he was to be guarded by the soldiers of the Praetorian Guard. There was usually a rota of guardsmen assigned to guard the prisoner. A chain was tied to Paul's wrist and to that of the soldier so that escape was impossible. It is most likely that every soldier in the entire palace guard had an opportunity of guarding Paul. These soldiers would hear Paul preach and talk to his friends. And when there was no one else in the room except Paul and the guard, Paul would converse with him, telling him about Jesus Christ for whose cause he was imprisoned. He tells the Philippians: '. . . As a result the whole palace guard and all the others here know that I am in prison because I am a servant of Christ' (Phil. 1:13).

Had Paul gone to Spain he would not have had a chance of preaching in the corridors of power. His imprisonment gave him the privilege of preaching to the finest regiment of the Roman army, the Imperial Guard. We know that some of the soldiers accepted Jesus Christ as their Lord and Saviour. At the conclusion of his letter to the Philippians, Paul says: 'All God's people here send greetings, especially those who belong to the Emperor's palace' (Philp. 4:22).

3. It was in his Roman prison cell that Paul dictated his so called 'Captivity Epistles'. These include Ephesians, Philippians, Colossians and Philemon. It is also certain that the Second Letter of Paul to Timothy was written from prison in Rome.

Who can imagine the New Testament without the Pauline letters and especially the great Captivity Epistles? It is in these letters that the theology of Paul is crystallized. The doctrine of salvation by grace through faith is to be found in the letter to the Ephesians. In the same letter Paul reaches the zenith of his meditation on Christian marriage and gives it the dignity it deserves.

The letter of Paul to Philippians is called the Epistle of Joy. This is because the word joy occurs more in this letter than in any other of Paul's epistles. It is difficult to imagine that it was a man in a prison cell guarded by a soldier who wrote to his friends these lovely words,

> Rejoice in the Lord always. I will say it again, Rejoice! Let your gentleness be evident to all. The Lord is near. Do not be anxious about anything, but in everything by prayer and petition with thanksgiving, present your requests to God.

> And the peace of God which transcends all understanding will guard your hearts and your minds in Christ Jesus [Philp. 4:4–7].

It is in the letter to the Colossians that Paul's Christology reaches its climax. To Paul, 'Christ is the image of the invisible God, the first-born of all creation. For by him all things were created: things in heaven and on earth, visible and invisible, whether thrones or powers or rulers or authorities; all things were created by him and for him. He is before all things and in him all things hold together' (Col. 1:15:17).

Had St Paul gone to Spain he would possibly not have had the time to meditate and to write these great epistles. Indeed we can give thanks to God for Paul's imprisonment, and further be thankful to Paul for this great lesson: that you can turn a seemingly great liability to an equally great asset. To this day we are encouraged and enriched as we read the Captivity Epistles. There is no doubt that conditions in the Roman jail enabled Paul to achieve what he did. Though he was a prisoner, his friends were allowed to visit him regularly and without any hindrance. He was also allowed to have his books as well as writing materials. He tells Timothy, 'When you come, bring my coat that I left in Troas with Carpus; bring the books too, and especially the ones made of parchment' [2 Tim. 4:13].

Conclusion

When, like Paul, we learn to face our shattered hopes with courage, we shall find peace, the true peace that transcends all understanding. We often tend to relate peace with absence of pain or trouble, when there are no storms in life. However, the peace which Paul spoke of is, 'calmness of heart amid terrors of trouble; inner tranquility amid the raging storm; one severe quiet in the midst of a hurricane. True peace is calm that exceeds all descriptions and all explanations. It is peace amid storm and tranquillity amid disaster'.

Our capacity to deal with our shattered dreams is ultimately determined by our faith in God. Genuine faith gives us the conviction that beyond time is a divine spirit and beyond life is life. However dismal and catastrophic the present circumstances, we know we are not alone, for God dwells in life's most confusing and oppressive cell. Even if we die before reaching 'Spain', we shall reach that City of God where we shall receive the crown of glory. Our earthly life is prelude to a glorious new awakening, and death is the door into life eternal.

The Christian faith makes it possible for us to accept nobly that which cannot be changed, to meet disappointment and sorrow with an inner poise, to bear the most intense pain without abandoning our sense of hope. For we know, as Paul testified, that in Spain or in Rome, all things work together for good to them that love God, those whom he has called according to his purpose

Why should you spend all your time focusing on what you consider to be your liabilities? Turn them to assets and glorify God with your talents. Paul prayed three times that his thorn might be removed from him but the Lord's reply was, No! '. . . for my power is made perfect in weakness'. Paul could then rejoice in the fact that '. . . when I am weak, then I am strong' (2 Cor. 12:10).

Glory Be to God!

3

Crisis Count Down

Preached at Kenyatta University College during the Mission to University Students, November 1978.

THE SERMON

'Then the disciples came to Jesus in private and asked him, "Why couldn't we drive the demon out?" ' [Mt. 17:19].

Human life through the centuries has been characterized by the persistent effort to remove evil from the world. Seldom have people completely accepted evil, for inspite of their realizations and compromises, they know that the 'is' is not the 'ought' and the ideal is not possible.

Though the evils of sensuality, selfishness and cruelty often rise aggressively in our souls, something within tells us that they are intruders and reminds us of our higher destiny and a nobler allegiance. When one's conscience is alive it often reminds one that evil is a foreign invader that must be driven from the native soil of the soul before one can achieve moral and spiritual dignity.

But the problem that has worried humanity is our inability to conquer evil by our own power. In pathetic amazement we ask, 'Why can I not cast it out? Why can I not remove this evil from my life?' This agonizing and perplexing question recalls an event that occurred immediately after Christ's transfiguration.

Coming down the mountain Jesus found a small boy who was in convulsions. His disciples had tried desperately to cure the unhappy child but the more they laboured the more they realized their inadequacies and the pathetic limitations of their power. When they were just about to give up in despair, the Lord appeared on the scene, and the boy's father rushed to him; 'I brought (the boy) to your disciples', he said, 'but they could not heal him'. Then Jesus rebuked the demon and from that very hour the child was cured. When the disciples were finally alone with Jesus, they asked him, 'Why could we not cast it out?' The disciples wanted an explanation of their limitations. And Jesus told them their failure was caused by their unbelief. 'If you have faith as a grain of mustard seed, nothing will be impossible . . .', he said. Martin Luther King Jr. in his book *Strength To Love*, says,

They had tried to do by themselves what could be done only after they had surrendered their natures to God so as to enable his strength to flow freely through them.

How Can Evil be Removed?

Humanity has usually pursued two paths to eliminate evil and thereby save the world. We try to remove evil by our own power and integrity because of our strange conviction that, by thinking, by human inventions and by government, we will at last conquer the persistent forces of evil. It is often said, 'Give people a fair chance, a decent education and they will save themselves'. This idea sweeping across the modern world like a plague has driven God out, ushered humanity in and has substituted human ingenuity for divine guidance. This probably resulted from the dawning of the Enlightenment when reason dethroned religion; or later when Darwin's *Origin of Species* replaced belief in creation with the theory of evolution; or when the Industrial Revolution in Europe turned the hearts of people to material comforts and physical conveniences. The idea of the adequacy of humanity to solve the evils of history captured the minds of people, giving rise to the easy optimism of the doctrine of the inevitable progress of humanity.

It was popularly believed that human advancement would make the world a utopia. 'By human reason alone', it was argued, 'the whole world will soon be cleansed of crime, poverty and war'. Hegel expounded an evolutionary view of the universe, according to which the logic of world history was inexorably realizing itself through the dialectical process of thesis, antithesis and synthesis. Karl Marx tried to prove the possibility of a kind of utopia on earth. Spencer said, 'It is certain that man must become perfect'. Armed with this growing faith in the capability of reason and science, modern man set out to change the world. He turned his attention from God and the human soul to the world and its possibilities. Man observed, analyzed, and explored. The laboratory became man's sanctuary and scientists his priests and prophets; as one modern humanist has written:

> The future is not with the Churches but with the laboratories, not with prophets but with scientists, not with piety but with efficiency. Man is at last becoming aware that he alone is responsible for the realization of the world of his dreams, that he has within himself the power to achieve it.

There is no doubt that scientific laboratories have brought unbelievable advances in power and comfort, producing machines that think and vessels that soar majestically through the skies, stand impressively on the land, and move with stately dignity on the seas. But in spite of all this, evil continues to dominate and the age of reason has become the age of terror. Selfishness and hatred have not vanished with the enlargement of our educational system and extension of our legislative policies. The difficult times which St Paul predicted seems to have come. He wrote: 'Remember this! There will be difficult times in the last days, for men will be selfish, greedy, boastful and conceited – they will be insulting, disobedient to their parents, ungrateful and irreligious. They will be unkind, merciless, slanderers, violent and fierce. They will hate good, they will be treacherous, reckless, swollen with pride, they will love pleasure rather than God' [2 Tim.3:1–4].

A person, by his or her own power cannot cast evil out of the world. The humanist's hope is an illusion, based on too great an optimism concerning the inherent goodness of human nature. It is futile for a human being to seek salvation within the human context. Those who put their trust in humanity were disillusioned; for when they thought they were moving towards Utopia, the first World War broke out and was closely followed by the second World War. Terrible things were done, including the slaughter of six million Jews by the Nazi regime of Adolf Hitler. Humanistic optimism ignored the fundamental facts of our fallen human nature. Science has lifted us from the stagnating valleys of superstition and half truths to the sun-lit mountains of appraisal. But the exalted Renaissance optimism, while attempting to free the mind, forgot about humanity's major crisis, our capacity to sin! There is no way in which this crisis can be overcome by science or technology. And so, whether scientists like it or not, God must be ushered in and be accorded his rightful place at the centre of human life. The role of the Church, the prophets and priests, can never be undervalued.

Total Submission to God

'In his own good time the Lord will redeem the world.' So argue the proponents of another doctrine which seems to deny completely the capability of sinful humanity to do anything about ourselves. The Reformation seems to have pushed this doctrine too far. While the Renaissance was too optimistic about the nature of man, the Reformation was too pessimistic. The Renaissance concentrated so much on the goodness of mankind that it overlooked our inclination towards evil. On the other hand, Reformation concentrated so much on the wickedness of human nature that it overlooked our capacity for goodness. While rightly affirming the sinfulness of human nature and our incapacity to save ourselves, the Reformation may have wrongly affirmed that the image of God had been completely erased from humanity.

Even though humanity fell through disobedience, the image of God in us was not completely erased, only blurred. There are some sections of the Church which have stressed the utter hopelessness of this world and called upon the individual to concentrate solely on preparing his soul for the world to come.

By ignoring the need for social reform, religion is divorced from the mainstream of human life. Christianity is not just meant for the soul; it is for the whole person. The Bible knows nothing about an isolated soul, for Man is 'body', 'mind', and 'soul'. He is a psychosomatic unit. Even in salvation it is not just the soul which is (or should be) saved; it is the whole person; further, the change is not just for the individual; it is for the whole society. By disregarding the psychosomatic approach of the gospel, this one-sided emphasis creates a strange dichotomy between the sacred and the secular. The Church must seek to transform both individual lives and the social situations that bring to many people anguish of spirit and cruel bondage.

In the gospels, there is a threefold summary of the mission of Jesus: teaching , preaching and healing. We read: 'So Jesus went around visiting all towns and villages. He taught in their synagogues, preached the Good News of the Kingdom and healed people from every kind of disease and sickness' [Mt. 9:35].

When we expect God to do everything, this inevitably leads to prayer without commitment. For if God does everything, then all we have to do is to wait for the answer. Although every true Christian should pray for God's help and guidance in his or her life, we must also rise up in the power of prayer and confront the evil in the world. God has given us a mind for thinking and working. When we pray he gives us directions to follow, and the power to confront evil in the world.

We have to co-operate with God in bringing about a just, united, peaceful and liberated nation. The Church is not merely meant to pray for the long life of those in authority. More importantly, it must keep reminding them of the righteousness that God requires.

Politicians have often cautioned Church leaders to keep out of politics, arguing that it is a dirty game. But isn't a game made dirty by players who are themselves dirty? Politics is about the welfare of the people and it is ridiculous for the politicians to expect Church leaders to remain in an ivory tower, and merely spectate. There is no way that we can do this. We are sailing in the same boat, and if anything goes wrong with the boat we shall all be affected. Martin Luther King Jr., the great Churchman who led the Civil Rights movement in America, once told his people:

> We must pray unceasingly for racial justice, but we must also use our minds to develop a programme, organise ourselves into mass non-violent action, and employ every resource of our bodies and souls to bring an end to racial injustice. We must pray unrelentingly for economic justice, but we must work diligently to bring into being those social changes that make for a better distribution of wealth within our nation and in underdeveloped countries of the World (Martin Luther King Jr. *Strength to Love*).

During the Lausanne Congress on World Evangelization, held in 1974, an important statement was made on Christian participation in socio-political activities, to the effect that man is not just expected to sit and wait for God to come and cast out the evil from the world.

No prodigious thunderbolt from heaven will blast away evil. No mighty army of angels will physically descend and force people to do what they should, against their will. The Bible portrays God not as an omnipotent dictator who makes all decisions for his subjects, nor as a cosmic tyrant who, with gestapo-like methods, invades the inner lives of people, but rather as a loving father who gives to his children such abundant blessings as they may be willing to receive – we ourselves must do something. . . .

People are not left helpless in a valley of total depravity until God pulls them out. Each of us is an upstanding human being whose vision has been impaired by the cataracts of sin and whose soul has been weakened by a virus of pride; but there is sufficient vision left for us to lift our eyes to the hills, and there remains enough of God's image in us for us to turn with our weak and sin-battered lives towards the great physician, the curer of the ravages of sin.

The real weakness in the idea that God will do everything is its false conception of both God and man. It makes God so absolutely sovereign that men and women are absolutely helpless. It makes them so absolutely depraved that they can do nothing except to wait upon God. This view makes God a despotic dictator instead of the loving father that he is. It ends up with such a pessimistic view of human nature, that it makes people look like helpless worms crawling through the morass of an evil world. But humanity is not totally depraved, nor is God an almighty dictator.

We must affirm the majesty and sovereignty of God. Yet this should not lead us to see God as an almighty monarch who will impose his will upon us and deprive us of the freedom to choose between good and evil. He will not thrust himself upon us nor force us to stay at home when we have already made up our minds to go to the distant country of sin. But he will follow us in love and when we come back to ourselves and turn our tired feet back to the father's house, he stands waiting with outstretched arms of love and forgiveness.

The Problem of Evil

If God is a God of love, how can he allow so much suffering in his creation? How can we possibly reconcile the presence of evil with the concept of a God who is all-wise, all-powerful, and all-loving? There is no conclusive answer.

Evil is inherent in the gift of free will with its attendant risks. Naturally it was possible for God to make creatures who were invariably good, healthy, kind and virtuous. But if they had no chance to do anything else, that is, if they had no free will, such creatures would have been no more than characterless robots. The individual gift to choose good and evil affects a far wider area of human life than that of one individual personality. The choices that people make between good or evil have immediate as well as long term effects, and exert an influence for better or for worse. Good produces happiness, Evil produces misery and suffering.

A good deal of humanity's suffering can therefore be traced to the evil choices of people. For instance, a violent husband causes suffering, fear and misery to his wife and children. Sometimes evil is indirect, where greed for wealth or power may lead a businessman to take decisions which may bring great suffering to hundreds of people who are personally unknown to him. Selfishness and greed in one generation can produce bitter fruits in the next. Natural catastrophes as well as man-made catastrophes such as wars often lead us to question whether there was any point in creating the world in the first place.

A Christian must be committed to do all in his power to heal the world's injuries, notwithstanding the high personal cost. But all the time he enjoys the enormous advantage of knowing that even the most hideous suffering exists only in this present world. He waits in hope for a new creation, as St Paul says:

> I consider the sufferings of this present time are not worth comparing with the glory that is to be revealed to us. For creation waits with eager longing for the revealing of the sons of God: for the creation was subjected to futility, not of its own will but by the will of him who subjected it in hope; because the creation itself will be set free from its bondage to decay and obtain the glorious liberty of the children of God. We know that the whole creation has been groaning in travail together until now and not only creation but we ourselves . . . groan inwardly as we wait the adoption as sons for redemption of our bodies, for in this hope we are saved [Rom. 8:18–25].

We should never expect that God will, through some breathtaking miracle, cast evil out of the world. The belief that God will do everything for you while you sit and wait is as untenable as the belief that man can do everything for himself. It is not faith; it is, at best, superstition.

God and Man Working Together

How can evil be cast out of our individual and collective lives? Both God and people, made one in a marvellous unity of purpose through an overflowing love on God's part, and by perfect obedience and receptivity on the part of people, can transform the old into the new, and remove the deadly cancer of sin.

The principle which opens the door for God to work through people is faith. This is what the disciples lacked when they tried desperately to cast out the demon from the little boy. Jesus reminded them that they were attempting to do by themselves what could be done only when their lives were open to the free outpouring of God's power. Faith is not just believing the basic principles of Christian faith; it is the opening on all sides, and at every level, of one's life to the divine inflow.

Paul taught the doctrine of salvation by faith. For him faith is our capacity to accept God's willingness through Christ to rescue us from the bondage of sin. God freely offers to do for us what we cannot do for ourselves. Our humble and open hearted acceptance is faith. 'For by grace you have been saved through faith, and this is not your own doing, it is the gift of God – not because of works lest anyone should boast' [Eph. 2:8–9]. 'Work out your own salvation with fear and trembling for God is always at work in you, both to make you willing and able to obey his own purpose' [Philp. 2:12b–13].

So by faith we are saved! People filled with God and God operating through people brings wonderful changes in our individual and social lives. Social evils have trapped multitudes of men and women in a dark and murky corridor with no exit sign, and has plunged others into psychological fatalism.

These deadly evils can be removed by a humanity perfectly united through obedience to God. Moral victory will come as God fills us and as we open up our life by faith to God. 'If any man thirsts', Jesus said, 'let him come to me and drink – he who believes in me, as the Scriptures say, out of him shall flow rivers of living water' [Jn. 7:38]. Others will drink from these living waters and find joy, satisfaction and fulfillment. Martin Luther King further wrote:

> Racial justice, a genuine possibility in our nation and in the world, will come neither by our frail and often misguided efforts, nor by God imposing his will on wayward men, but when enough people open their lives to God to allow him pour his triumphant, divine energy into their souls. Our age old and noble dream of a world of peace may yet become a reality but it will come neither by man working alone nor by God destroying the wicked schemes of men, but when men so open their lives to God that he may fill them with love, mutual respect and understanding, and goodwill. (*Strength To Love*)

Many of you know what it means to struggle with sin. Year by year, day by day, you know in your own life the struggle you have with a particular sin, and how, as life goes on you realize this is not as it should be. You want freedom but you find you are still a slave of these besetting sins. Many times you have made a resolution to drive out the sin but it persists. How frustrating! You have failed because you tried through your own effort. You still ask; 'Why could I not cast it out?'

God has promised to co-operate with us when we seek to cast evil from our lives and become true children of his divine will. 'If any one is in Christ, he is a new creation, the old has passed away, behold the new has come.' One of the greatest glories of the gospel is that Christ has changed numerous prodigals:

He changed Simon of sand into Peter the rock;
A persecuting Saul into the apostle Paul;
A lust-loving Augustine into Saint Augustine.

These and many more great men and women of faith opened up to the Lord and he came into their lives: 'Behold I stand at the door and knock – if any man hears my voice and opens the door, I will come in to him, and will sup with him and he with me' [Rev. 3:20]. When we open the door of our hearts in faith, a divine and human encounter transforms our sin-ruined lives into radiant personalities. Amen.

4

Who Knows . . . ?

Esther 4:14b

Preached two weeks prior to the Attempted Coup of August 1 1982

THE SETTING

Formerly in the Diocese of Mt Kenya East, and even now in Kirinyaga Diocese, we always celebrate the anniversary of the diocese. In this case the 7th Anniversary was celebrated at St Andrew's Church, Kiamaina during which we also consecrated the Church which was the largest so far. The ceremony was graced by, among others, Hon. Jeremiah Nyaga, a cabinet minister; Mr David Musila, the Provincial Commissioner Central Province; Mr Geoffrey Kariithi, a former permanent secretary in the office of the President and head of the Civil Service; heads of institutions of learning, and several other dignitaries.

At this time the political situation in the country was rather volatile as parliament had earlier passed a bill to make Kenya a de jure *one party state in a motion that was hastily passed in a session of only about 45 minutes. This was meant to hinder Mr Oginga Odinga, a staunch politician and government critic, who was at one time Vice-President under the late Jomo Kenyatta, from forming another political party as he had threatened to do, together with another fiery legislator, George Anyona. The latter was soon after arrested and detained without trial. The haste with which the constitution was changed did not augur well for the peace of the nation. It was under these circumstances that the Bishop chose to preach a sermon from the Book of Esther during the service which was attended by about two thousand people.*

THE SERMON

The theme of my sermon today is taken from a verse in Chapter 4 of the book of Esther. 'And who knows but that you have come to your royal position for such a time as this . . . ?'

This was a question posed by Mordecai, a cousin of Esther, a Jewess who had just been crowned the Queen of Persia. Although a Jew, Mordecai was also to hold an important post in the king's palace. Esther had become the queen at a very critical time, as there was a plot to exterminate all the Jews in the Persian empire.

Discredited and Divorced Queen Vashti

If you've never had enough interest to read the Book of Esther, I would encourage you to go and read it, as it is one of the most interesting Bible stories. Esther is one of the five festal scrolls that are read even now at important Jewish festivals. Despite the fact that it does not have a single explicit reference to God or the religious practices of Judaism, the book of Esther came to be regarded as the Scroll *par excellence*.

The story is placed during the reign of King Ahasuerus or Xerxes I who was king of Persia and Media (486 to 465BC). He ruled over 127 Provinces which extended from India to the Upper Nile region.

The scene opens in his winter palace at Susa where he throws a banquet for all his nobles and officials. The banquet lasted about 180 days (six months), and was attended by military leaders from Persia and Media; by princes and nobles and many diplomats. From what we read in chapter 1, this was a very lavish feast. 'Wine was served in goblets of gold, each one different from the other, and the royal wine was different, in keeping with the King's liberality. By the King's command, each guest was allowed to drink in his own way for the King had instructed all the stewards to serve each man whatever he wished' (Est. 1:7–8). Cocktail parties are not a recent invention.

The King's wife, Vashti, also threw a banquet for the women in the State House. We are told that on the seventh day when the King was in high spirits from much wine, he commanded the seven eunuchs who served him, to bring before him Queen Vashti wearing her royal crown, in order to display her beauty to the people, and all the nobles, for she was very lovely to look at (1: 11). But to the King's dismay the Queen refused to appear. The King had regarded Vashti as his most precious treasure and he wanted to bring this great feast to a climax by displaying her beauty. And so, her refusal to come so humiliated the King before his dignitaries, that he became furious and burst out in anger. No reason is given for the Queen's refusal to obey the King.

The King then consulted experts in matters of law and justice and Vashti was condemned in a hurriedly convened court by drunken wise men. She was not given a chance to defend herself and the all-male court advised the King to issue a royal decree that, 'Vashti is never again to enter the presence of King Xerxes'. The state machinery was to be put into force to look for a replacement for Vashti. The court further advised the King to issue an edict throughout his vast empire that all women should respect their husbands from the least to the greatest. The court was composed of seven so-called wise men. Note that there was no woman to represent the women's viewpoints. The meeting also seems to have been dominated by one man called Memucan. 'According to the law, what must be done to Queen Vashti?', the question was asked. We read in chapter 1:16 that Memucan replied thus in the presence of the king and the nobles: 'Queen Vashti has done wrong not only against the King but also against all the nobles and the people of all the

Provinces of King Xerxes. For the Queen's conduct will become known to all the women and so they will despise their husbands and say, "King Xerxes commanded Queen Vashti to be brought before him but she would not." '

Apparently the views of Memucan were not debated and were accepted within a few minutes. Indeed we read that 'the King and the nobles were pleased with his advice, so the King did as Memucan proposed' [1: 21].

Memucan's appeal to male self-interest won the support of both the King and his Princes. 'By depicting the King dispatching his edict without so much as a further thought, the author comments on the whimsical way laws were made in a land which made so much of law and judgement.'

Are we Kenyans not making similar mistakes today? On 9th June 1982 the bill to make Kenya a *de jure* one-party state passed through parliament in only 45 minutes. History will judge whether the hasty decision made by parliament to change the constitution, thus making it illegal for anyone to form another party, was right or not. Such major changes require an open debate by people of all walks of life for a considerable period of time before parliament has the right to take over and decide what are the wishes of the people.

Much later, after King Xerxes' anger had subsided, the King remembered Vashti, what she had done, and his decree concerning her (Est. 2:1). It is most likely that the King regretted the hasty decision which made him lose his wife. But he could not reverse the decision since the laws of Persia and Media could not be repealed. However, the laws of Kenya can be changed; and we look forward to the day when the mistake made on 9th June 1982 will be rectified through the removal of Clause 2A of our constitution.

Esther Becomes Queen of Persia and Media

Following Vashti's divorce, we hear that the whole empire was mobilized in search of a beauty to replace her. 'Then the King's personal attendants proposed, "Let a search be made for beautiful young virgins for the King. Let the king appoint commissioners in every Province of his realm to bring all these beautiful girls into the harem in the citadel of Susa." ' [Est. 2:2–3].

It appears as if beauty contests were held in each of the 127 Provinces, after which the winners were brought to Susa for the final contest. The winners were kept under the care of Hegai, the king's Eunuch. The girls had to complete twelve months of beauty treatment (six months with oil of myrrh, and six with perfumes and cosmetics). They were also given special food. After this, each beauty was sent before the King who had to make the final choice.

Mordecai, a Jew of the tribe of Benjamin and living in the citadel of Susa, encouraged his cousin Esther to join the contest. Esther who was lovely in form and features had been adopted by Mordecai following her mother's death. Esther won the provincial beauty contest and thus qualified for the major contest at the King's palace. She was entrusted to Hegai who was so impressed by her striking beauty that he assigned to her seven maids selected from the King's palace and she was given very special treatment.

When it was Esther's turn to appear before the King he was immediately attracted to her and so she won the King's favour and approval more than any of the other virgins. Consequently Esther was crowned Queen of Persia and the Medes and the King gave a great banquet in honour of the new Queen, and distributed gifts with royal liberality. A national holiday was declared throughout the empire. But Esther, on the advice of Mordecai, never disclosed that she was a Jewess.

Mordecai Unearths a Coup Plot

Two watchmen who guarded the King's gates made a secret plot to assassinate the King. But Mordecai discovered the plot and reported it to Queen Esther who in turn told the King. When the matter was investigated and found to be true, the two officials were summarily hanged at the gallows and the credit for the discovery of the plot went to Mordecai.

Plot To Destroy Jews

After Esther became Queen, King Xerxes honoured Haman son of Hammedatha by elevating him to the position of Prime Minister. Whenever the Prime Minister was passing by, all the royal officials at the King's gates were expected to kneel in his honour. But Mordecai persistently refused to kneel down or to pay him honour. This enraged the Prime Minister, especially when he realized that Mordecai was a Jew. His anger was so great that he began planning how he would kill not only Mordecai but all the Jews in the empire. By casting lots the Prime Minister decided the massacre of the Jews would take place on the 12th month of Adar. He then decided to seek the King's blessing for this plan.

Haman presented his project to the King in a subtle mixture of truth, half truth and outright lies. He told the King: 'There is a certain people dispersed and scattered among the peoples in all the Provinces of your kingdom who keep themselves separate from those of all other people (half truth) and they do not obey the King's laws (a lie). It is not in the King's interest to tolerate them. If it pleases the King, let a decree be issued to destroy them and I will put ten thousand talents into the royal treasury for the men who carry out this business' (Est. 3:8–9).

Presuming that the scattered people in question were distant aliens, hostile to his cause, the King handed over his royal authority to Haman. His signet ring was the seal of executive power, recognized throughout the empire. Haman now had a free hand to kill about forty thousand Jews in the empire in a single day. The royal secretaries were summoned. 'They wrote out in the script of each Province and in the language of each people all Haman's orders to the King's satraps, the governors of various peoples. These were written in the name of King Xerxes and sealed with his own ring' (Est. 3:12). The order was to 'destroy, kill and annihilate all the Jews, young and old, on a single day – the thirteenth day of the twelfth month, the month of Adar, and to plunder their goods'. Having sent these dispatches with the edict to every Province the Prime Minister visited the King and they both sat down for a drink. The city of Susa was bewildered.

Earlier in the story the King had taken the advice of a few drunken men and got rid of his wife Vashti without attempting any investigation of her behaviour. Now we see the King hurrying to authorize the deaths of tens of thousands of his citizens by heeding the advice of one power-hungry prime minister. In the process he stood to lose his new wife Esther because she was also a Jew.

The kings of this world must be careful about rushing to accept every recommendation made by those surrounding them in their palaces. Where human life is at stake, a very thorough investigation must be undertaken to establish the truth beyond any reasonable doubt. Realizing that a major crime against the Jewish community was in the offing, Mordecai tore his clothes, put on sackcloth and ashes and went out into the city wailing loudly and bitterly. Esther heard from the maids that Mordecai was in sackcloth and for that she was greatly distressed. She sent clothes to him but he rejected them. She then sent out somebody to find out what the problem was. Mordecai told Hathach the messenger everything, including the exact amount of money Haman was going to pay to the royal treasury for the extermination of the Jews. Esther was also given a copy of the text of the edict for the annihilation of the Jews. Mordecai asked Hathach to urge Esther to go in to the King's presence to beg for mercy and plead with him for her people.

In reply Esther sent a message to Mordecai to say that it was very dangerous to approach the King in the inner court unless she was summoned by him. It was now thirty days since she had been called into the presence of the King. When Mordecai saw that the Queen did not realize the seriousness and the urgency of this matter, he sent yet another message:

> Do not think that because you are in the King's house you alone of all the Jews will escape, for if you remain silent at this time, relief and deliverance for the Jews will arise from another place, but you and your father's family will perish. And who knows but that you have come to your royal position for such a time as this? [Est. 4: 13–14].

On receiving this message Esther asked Mordecai to gather together all the Jews who were in Susa to fast and pray for her as she prepared to see the King, even though it was against the law. As a result of three days of fasting and prayer by all the Jews in Susa and Esther herself and her maids, she took courage to go and see the King in the inner courts of the Palace.

When the King saw her he welcomed her but she did not hurry to explain her concern. Instead, she asked permission to prepare a banquet for the King and the Prime Minister. Permission was granted and the King and the Prime Minister had a wonderful dinner and plenty to drink. But Esther did not reveal her message at that time; rather, she requested the two to come for another banquet the following day. Haman went home in high spirits and called his wife and friends to tell them how he had been honoured by the King and the Queen. He boasted about his vast wealth, his many sons, the honours he had received from the King, and how he had been elevated above all the other nobles and officials. However, he emphatically stated that all that did not give him satisfaction as 'long as I see that Jew Mordecai sitting at the King's gate'.

His wife and friends advised him to build gallows seventy feet high, and ask the King in the morning to have Mordecai hanged on it, 'then go with the King to the dinner and be happy'. The suggestion delighted the Prime Minister and he had the gallows built. Meanwhile the King wanted to honour the man who had unearthed the conspiracy to have him assassinated. And that was none other than Mordecai. The King ordered a royal robe to be put on Mordecai and to lead him on a horse through the city streets proclaiming before him, 'This is what is done for the man the King delights to honour'.

After the banquet on the second day, Esther had the courage to request the King to save the Jews and revealed Haman's involvement in the plot. The King was enraged with the action of his Prime Minister and ordered him to be hanged on the same gallows he had built for Mordecai. The King then nullified the former orders and a new edict granted Jews in every city the right to assemble and protect themselves, to destroy, kill and annihilate any armed force of any nationality or province that might attack them. There was joy, gladness and celebration wherever the King's edict was read.

Conclusion

'And who knows but that you have come to your royal position for such a time as this? Only do not keep silent.' There are people present here at this occasion who are holding important positions in society. It may be that God has placed you in that position for such a time as this. There are those of you who are in administrative government posts, like our PC Mr David Musila. Indeed some of you have direct access to the President of the land, in which case you can say a word to him that could promote peace and the welfare of the nation, and possibly avert looming disaster. Only do not keep quiet.

We also have with us parliamentarians and even a cabinet minister. You are elected by the people so that you might represent their concerns to the highest decision-making body in the land. Your greatest concern should be to promote justice and peace but some of the leaders sing 'peace, peace, peace,' when there is no peace. And who knows but that you have come to your 'royal' position for such a time as this; only do not keep silent when things seem to be going wrong. Take courage during parliamentary sessions or during cabinet meetings, and correct your fellow leaders when they behave in unjust ways. The continued corruption and land-grabbing by some influential people does not work for peace. As a peacemaker, you are not supposed to keep quiet when things are going wrong.

You may be a member of the armed forces in the military, air force or navy. If you discover that some of your colleagues are planning to change the government through the unconstitutional use of military action, you must not keep quiet. Many African countries have had their governments changed by force, but we have been fortunate in that Kenya is one of the very few countries that have never experienced change of the government in that way. Indeed, we do not need a coup d'etat in Kenya. That however can be avoided only if we are willing to work for justice and peace and if we care for the welfare of the poor and the disadvantaged. All of us, whoever we are, should consider ourselves as instruments of peace, only we must not keep silent when the peace is being threatened by circumstances. If you keep silent do not think that you yourself will be safe. God can always bring help from elsewhere. However, he wants to use you. Only do not remain silent! AMEN

THE AFTERMATH OF THE SERMON

After the sermon the Provincial Commissioner of the Central Province, Mr David Musila was requested to address the gathering, during which he

congratulated the people of Kiamaina for having built such a magnificent Church. He also assured the congregation that there was peace in the country and that the government was in full control of the situation. The following day the newspapers reported only what the PC said.

Two weeks later on 1st August 1982, there was an attempted coup-de-tat! A large number of militia from the Air Force attempted to overthrow the government. The Voice of Kenya broadcasting station was taken over briefly and an announcement was made very early on that Sunday morning that the government was now in the hands of the armed forces and also ordering the police force to remain in their stations and not to move (and stay in civilian clothes).

Hell broke loose in the city of Nairobi as people went on a looting spree, mainly aiming at Asian shops. Several people died in the course of the scuffles that characterized the one day coup but by the end of the day the coup plotters had been cornered by the military forces and the coup bid thus foiled. The Kenya Air Force was eventually dissolved and a new Force put in place.

The Bishop's prophetic sermon was a timely warning. The preacher must never underrate the importance of preaching prophetically. He must also preach as if he were preaching his last sermon. He must therefore tell the congregation everything that God has put in his heart.

'God Bless Africa, Guard her children, Guide her leaders and give her peace. For Jesus Christ's sake,' Amen.

5

Blessed are the Peacemakers

Live Broadcast from All Saints Cathedral Nairobi on 3rd October 1982

THE SETTING

On 1st August 1982 Kenya suffered a shattering blow when elements of the Kenya Air Force staged an attempted coup. However, within 24 hours the rebels had been overcome but the fabric of national life was left seriously damaged. All national leaders in both Church and state co-operated to restore public confidence and to provide guidance to the people at this confusing time.

The rebels had briefly captured the Voice of Kenya radio station in Nairobi. But the station was re-occupied by the royal troops a few hours later and word went out to the whole nation that the situation was under control. Intermittently the station played the song, Hapa Kenya Hakuna Matata ('Here in Kenya we have no problems') very ironical indeed.

The coup inevitably led Kenyans to re-examine the foundations of their national life and unity. It was the Bishop's conviction that the future of the country's peace and security were not in the mere assertion that 'hapa Kenya hakuna matata', but that peace would come only when we recognized genuine problems where they existed in our society and were willing to confront and overcome them. In other words we must be peacemakers not just peace lovers.

THE SERMON

1. Introduction

The Sermon on the Mount as recorded by Matthew begins with these words: 'Seeing the crowds he went up on the mountain and when he sat down his disciples came to him. And he opened his mouth. . . .'

It was the habit of the Jewish rabbi to sit down whenever he wanted to give official teaching to his students. The fact that Jesus sat down on this particular occasion meant that he wanted to give serious and official teaching. The detailed study of the Sermon on the Mount confirms the conviction that here we have the central document of the Christian faith, for Jesus opened his mouth to give a pronouncement of the greatest weight and importance. Tonight I would like to focus our attention on the seventh beatitude, 'Blessed are the peacemakers for they shall be called sons of God'.

2. True peace and false peace

The word 'peace' has been of great importance to the Kenyan nation ever since Independence. Indeed, the National Anthem includes a prayer for peace, when it says: 'May we dwell in unity, peace and liberty'. Moreover, the Nyayo philosophy is summarized first and foremost by the term 'peace', followed by the two others, 'love' and 'unity'.

After the shock of the events of August 1, the term 'peace' cannot be of mere academic, semantic or speculative interest. The need to preserve peace is an urgent concern to all Kenyans. But as Christians, we need to turn to the Bible to understand precisely what peace means, and who the peacemakers are. In John's Gospel, Jesus made a very clear distinction between false peace and authentic peace. To quote the Gospel, Jesus tells his disciples, 'Peace I leave with you; My peace I give you. Not as the world gives do I give to you. Let not your hearts be troubled, neither let them be afraid' (Jn. 14:27).

And so, according to Jesus, there is a peace that God gives. The world promises a false sense of peace; Jesus promises authentic peace. The peace which the world gives is, by and large, a momentary and illusory peace, which lasts for only a very short time. It is the kind of peace which comes from escaping the realities of life. It is like a man who, finding that there are many problems at home, takes refuge in alcohol. When he is drunk he forgets all his problems and enjoys momentary peace. But when he becomes sober, he returns to the same old problems. Escaping from the realities of life is not the way of peace.

It is possible to assume that peace has now been restored in Kenyan society because in every district and every constituency throughout the country, thousands of people have gone into the streets to demonstrate against the August 1 rebels and to shout 'Nyayo, Nyayo' in support of the government; but our demonstrations must go deeper than the mere shouting of slogans. The Jerusalem mob shouted 'Hosanna, Hosanna' in support of Jesus when he entered the city riding an ass on a Sunday morning two thousand years ago. But five days later the same Jerusalem mob shouted, 'Crucify him! Crucify him!'

It was good that nearly the whole population of the city of Nairobi turned up at Uhuru Park to condemn the August 1 rebels; but I would not be surprised if a good number of those who were shouting 'Nyayo, Nyayo', on that day had participated in the looting. It is right to proclaim 'Nyayo! Nyayo!' and even to preach the philosophy vigorously. But more importantly, we must do everything possible to preserve peace in our beloved country. Shouting 'Peace, Peace' when there is no peace is the method of the false prophets. Believing in authentic peace and working tirelessly to preserve it is the task of the peacemakers.

3. Peacemakers and peace-lovers

'Blessed are the peacemakers, for they will be called sons of God'. Peacemakers are not the people who run away from problems. Indeed, peacemakers are not necessarily peace-lovers. A peace-lover is a person who allows a dangerous situation to develop in the family, in the Church or in society, because he does not want to get into difficulties by dealing with potentially troublesome problems. Such a person may be called peaceable and a peace-lover, but he is certainly not a peacemaker: for the longer any potentially dangerous situation is allowed to continue, the more serious its consequences are likely to be, and the harder it will be to achieve a solution.

The beatitude says, 'Blessed is the peacemaker.' This is a person who is prepared to face difficulties, unpleasantness and trouble, in order to make peace. The peace of which this beatitude speaks is not the spurious peace which comes from evading the issue; it is the peace which comes from facing the issue, and being prepared to give everything in toil and in sacrifice which the situation demands. As the writer of Proverbs says: 'Someone who holds back the truth causes trouble, but the one who openly criticizes works for peace' (Prov. 10:10).

4. Peace in every area of life

The Hebrew word for peace is *shalom*. It is from *shalom* that we have the Kiswahili words *Salamu* and *Salama*. To this day the Jews greet one another by saying, '*Shalom*' – peace. *Shalom* describes perfect welfare, serenity, prosperity and happiness. *Shalom* describes right relationships. This is the true meaning of peace. In this respect, there are three spheres where man needs peace: within himself, with his fellow-men and with God.

a. Peace Within

As William Barclay says, 'Man is a walking civil war.' In other words, there is an ongoing struggle within an individual: it is the struggle caused when we want to do what is right and yet end up doing what is wrong. This is the struggle of which Paul wrote so movingly in Romans 7: 'For I do not do the good that I want; but the evil I do not want is what I do.' This is the internal civil war between the desires of the spirit and the desires of the flesh. In this struggle, victory is possible only when we allow Christ to have power over self so that we can say with St. Paul, 'I live, yet not I, but Christ liveth in me'. Blessed indeed is the man who is at peace with himself, in whom the contradictions are reconciled, the man whose inner battle has been stilled in the control of Christ.

b. Peace with Fellow Men

We live in a divided world, with its iron curtains, its lines of demarcation and its divisions between race and race, nation and nation, man and man. Here in our country, there is urgent need for peace between husbands and wives, between children and parents, between employers and employees, between Africans and Asians, between the rich and the poor, between the Kenya Army and the Kenya Air Force, between those who claim that they are the only ones who are truly Nyayo followers, and those who believe that they too are also Nyayo followers. At the Kanu headquarters there is need for peace between those who make contradictory statements concerning the affairs of the only political party we have. There is need for peace in the student world, the commercial world and the political world.

The starting point for a Christian in his search for the meaning of the word peace in this (Nyayo) philosophy must be the biblical *shalom*. In the Bible the word *shalom* may be defined as 'the state of things which comes about when God's will is being done'. But sin has entered into the world and God's will is not being done. When and where the will of God is not done, there you find the potential for explosions which disrupt peace.

The question we should be asking ourselves is whether we are doing God's will in the Church, in the commercial world and in the political world. The message of the gospel is that God has taken action in this world of disorder, to bring it back to its true and normal state. As Paul says, 'God is not the God of chaos but of peace.' So when Jesus is born into the world, the message of the angels is, '. . . on earth be peace among men with whom he is pleased' [Lk. 2:14b]. Jesus is the one in whom the will of God is perfectly done. Through him the world will be brought back to the way of peace from which it has strayed. To do the will of God on earth is to exercise justice in every aspect of our national life. Injustice is the great cause of strife among men; but when justice is done, the cause of peace is served.

There was a time when the rulers of Judah thought all was well in Judah but everything the leaders were doing was contrary to justice. And so a brave prophet emerged, whose name was Jeremiah, and he sternly rebuked the false prophets who used to earn their daily living through false prophecies, saying peace, peace when there was no peace. It was evident that there was no peace because Judah was not walking in obedience to Yahweh. Jeremiah challenged the people saying,

> Change the way you are living and stop doing the things you are doing. Be fair in your treatment of one another. Stop taking advantage of aliens, orphans and widows. Stop killing innocent people in this land. Stop worshipping other gods that will destroy you (Jer. 7:5–7).

The way of peace in Kenya, like it was in Judah, is justice and righteousness. As part of our self examination after the sad events of August 1, Kenyans should investigate where there has been injustice and seek to do what is just. The way of peace is for the powerful to beware the temptation of accumulating wealth by unfair means. The way of peace is for justice not only to be done in law courts but also to be seen to have been done. The way of peace is for Kanu elections to be conducted in a fair manner. It is not justice, when only certain people have access to Kanu membership cards which they distribute only to those they are sure will elect them.

The way of peace is genuine concern for the poor and the under-privileged in the country. The way of peace is not only to talk about human rights but also to genuinely safeguard those rights, including the protection of the right to life, right to personal liberty, the right to own property, right to freedom from arbitrary search, the freedom of expression and association. The way of peace is to promote our democratic heritage by just means at every stage.

We all want peace to be preserved in this nation. The way of peace is for peacemakers to be actively involved in peace making. To bring about peace on earth and peace among men, the peacemakers have to boldly proclaim the gospel of Jesus Christ, at all times struggling against all types of injustices wherever they may be found.

The peacemakers will be called sons of God because they are seeking to do God's will. Indeed this is the main thrust of our national anthem, 'Justice be our shield and defender . . .' When Justice shields and defends innocent persons in the court of law, there we promote peace! When Justice shields and defends those wishing to make use of their democratic right of free expression and association, there we promote peace! When again it defends and shields the poor and the under-privileged, peace is promoted. This is probably why the writer of Proverbs said:

> Righteousness makes a nation great; sin is a disgrace to any nation; Kings cannot tolerate evil, because justice is what makes a nation strong. When rulers are concerned with justice, the nation will be strong; But when they are concerned only with money they ruin their countries. If a ruler pays attention to false information all his officials will be liars. If a king defends the rights of the poor he will rule for a long time. A nation without God's guidance is a nation without order. Happy is the man who keeps God's law. (Extracts from Proverbs)

That is the way of peace. That is the biblical interpretation of the Nyayo philosophy.

c. Peace with God

Finally we cannot make peace among others unless we have God's peace in our own hearts. He who has God's peace in his heart is reconciled with God and has the assurance that his sins have been forgiven; his conscience does not disturb him because he has put things right with God in whom he has put his complete trust.

The concept of the peace of God should however not be misconstrued to mean absence of troubles and anxieties. Yet despite the problems that people experience in this world, the person who is at peace with God and with himself enjoys inner tranquility and serenity even in the midst of the storm. He has the peace that Jesus promised his disciples when he said, 'My peace I give to you'; it is the peace that Paul referred to as that which passeth all understanding. Let us then as peacemakers, go forth and struggle to bring about justice in the world, wherever we might be. Let us enter every sphere of Kenyan society; and be the salt of the earth and the light of the world.

And the peace of God which passeth all understanding will keep your hearts and minds in Christ Jesus. Shalom.

6

The Way of Peace

Philippians 4:1–9

Sermon preached on 28th July 1985 at Kerugoya during the 10th Anniversary celebrations of the Diocese of Mt Kenya East

THE SETTING

A long procession of clergy, Lay Readers, Church Army Staff, members of the Mothers' Union, among others wound its way through Kerugoya town to the site of the new unfinished St Thomas Church. Thousands of Christians from all over the Diocese packed the Church compound to take part in the outdoor service which was particularly graced by the presence of theologians from all over Africa who were attending a consultation of the Africa Theological Fraternity of which Bishop David is the chairman to this day.

We rejoiced as we recounted God's blessings. Certificates were awarded to some of the longest serving staff members whose hard work had made these achievements possible. Some of them have since gone to be with the Lord.

As we celebrated these ten great years it was not all joy because the ruling party's elections had just ended, and many people were very bitter at the way Kanu had so massively rigged the elections. There were many political divisions and Kirinyaga was not spared. The cause of justice and peace had been largely abused. In his sermon therefore the Bishop preached on the subject of Justice and Righteousness as the way of Peace in the nation, calling upon the clergy to preach the same, and national leaders to aspire to live by these virtues.

THE SERMON

The Epistle of Paul to the Philippians is called the Epistle of Joy. This is because the word joy occurs many times. Today is a day of joy as we celebrate ten great years of the existence of our Diocese. As such I thought it would be appropriate to preach from the Epistle of Joy.

In this passage we have noted that Paul's main motive in writing this letter was the immense love he had for the Christians at Philippi. He says,

'Therefore my brethren, whom I love and long for, my joy and crown, stand firm thus in the Lord, my beloved' (4:1). It is because he loves them and has a deep affection for them that he has the liberty to write this epistle and even to correct them where things are not right.

It is important to remember that criticism does not always mean hatred. If you really loved a person you would be failing in your duty if you did not correct him. But that correction must always be done with love and with all courtesy and humility. With that sincere love, Paul now turns to three important subjects: Unity, Patience, Peace.

1. Unity

Paul has received information that there is disunity in the Philippian Church. Euodia and Syntyche, prominent women leaders in the Church were becoming a stumbling block to the believers because of their disunity (4:2–3). There is no doubt that these were outstanding women leaders in this Church who had greatly laboured alongside Paul in planting the Church. But they quarrelled so much that the news of their disagreement had reached Paul in his prison cell hundreds of miles away. Because of his love for them and for the Church, Paul writes, urging them to unite. Disunity in the Church often leads to serious consequences. It breaches the peace; it hinders progress and it puts many people off.

This Diocese has made great progress during the last ten years. One of the secrets of our great success is that the Christians in this Diocese have been united behind their Bishop. The Gikuyu of Kirinyaga, the Wa-Embu and Wa-Mbeere of Embu District, the Wa-Meru of Meru District, the Wakamba of Karaba, the Gabbras and the Borans of Marsabit, all of us, have worked together to build a diocese where great things are happening. But we have not been completely free from elements of disunity.

Pockets of quarrelling by leaders have been found at parish and congregational levels. We thank God that these have not been widespread. If we had started arguing about where to build the cathedral or the Bible School, or Development offices, we would have continued arguing and nothing could have been achieved. But we had agreed from the very beginning that the cathedral would be built at Embu, the Bible School at Kabare and the Development offices here at Kerugoya, and then we got on with the job. That unity must be safeguarded if we want our Diocese to continue growing with the same or greater momentum.

Nevertheless we still have some leaders who are like Euodia and Syntyche. They do not see eye to eye. I urge them now, whoever they might be, to agree in the Lord. Unity is the key to the future of this Diocese. One day, I do not know when, the Diocese will probably be divided; let that day find us united in the Lord.

Wherever disunity exists, we must exercise the ministry of reconciliation. Paul urged one of the key Christian leaders in Philippi to play the role of reconciler of these two women. 'And you too my faithful partner. I want you to help these women' (4:3a). Church leaders are called upon to be reconcilers. Where people are disunited we are called upon to play our role in reconciling them. But Church leaders can never succeed in reconciling quarrelling groups if they are already prejudiced against one group or the other. In any kind of dispute, a reconciler must never be biased towards any one group. His bias must be only on the side of the truth.

It is common knowledge that in the Gichugu Division of Kirinyaga District, people are sharply divided between what has come to be known as *Twenty One* and *Forty Two*. Though they are members of one political party, within that party there are two contradictory philosophies which appear virtually irreconcilable. But reconciliation is not impossible and the Church leadership must play its part prayerfully in reconciling the people of Gichugu. But how can the Bishop or the Priest, or for that matter the Lay Reader reconcile *Twenty One* and *Forty Two* if he is himself an active member of one group or the other?

I (as the Bishop) together with all the Clergy, refuse to take sides on such matters so that we are in a position to play our role as reconcilers. The side we will take is the side of truth; and the truth will not necessarily be with any of these philosophical groupings. In one season the truth might be with the *Twenty One*; and the next season it might be with the *Forty Two*.

Since Lay Readers are the representatives of the Church at the local level, they too, like the Bishop and the Clergy, must not be permanently affiliated to one side, whether it is holding the truth or not. We want our Christians to be active in Politics, but the Lay Readers and the Clergy should not be involved with divisive party politics if they are going to be effective in reconciling *Euodia* and *Syntyche*. And so I urge you my faithful partner in the gospel – you the parish priest, you lay reader, to reconcile *Euodia* and *Syntyche*. But heed this; you cannot reconcile them if you are already biased.

2. Patience

Paul then tells the Philippians: 'Rejoice in the Lord always: again I say rejoice. Let all men know your forbearance (patience); the Lord is at hand.' The New Testament Greek word for patience is very informative. In this verse Paul tells us to have *epieikes* (forbearance), the patience that refrains from rushing to avenge a wrong or an insult.

Elsewhere he often uses two other Greek words for patience: *makrothumia* and *hupomone*. The latter is patience with things and circumstances. It is not the passive sitting and folding of arms and bearing things; it is the triumphant facing of circumstances so that even out of evil, good can come; out of failure, success. *Hupomone* describes not the spirit that accepts life as it is but a spirit which masters life. *Makrothumia* is patience not with things but with people. This is the quality that we who are called to lead others must be prepared to cultivate. We must be prepared to be patient with people, however unkind they might be.

In these last ten years, I have tried my best to be patient with those who work under me, and I have seen the results of that patience. In the face of trials and attacks we are called upon to rejoice in the Lord and to let all know our patience. After all we know that the Lord is near. It is like those disciples in a little boat in that stormy sea, who were filled with so much anxiety that they started to fear death. Yet the Lord of life, the creator of the sea and the wind was sleeping on a pillow in that same boat. He was incredibly near. And when he woke up he rebuked the sea. 'Peace be still', he commanded, and behold, the storm subsided.

Paul exhorts us to 'have no anxiety about anything, but in everything by prayer and supplication with thanksgiving, let your requests be made known to God'. This should be our motivating factor as we begin the next decade of our diocese.

3. Peace

Finally, Paul tells the Philippians, 'And the peace of God which passes all understanding will keep your hearts and your minds in Christ Jesus.' Note that Paul is speaking of the peace of God. This is because there can be a peace of the world which is only short lived. That is why the prophet Jeremiah told the rulers of Israel, 'You are saying "peace peace" when there is no peace' (Jer. 8:11b).

The people of Judah in Jeremiah's day thought that the temple was the guarantor of their peace: hence they used to say, 'This is the temple of the Lord, the temple of the Lord' (Jer. 7:4b). They thought the temple was enough to protect them from their enemies. We too can make our own temples – military powers, police force, the powers that be; and assume that they are sufficient to guarantee the nation's peace. This is not the way of peace. Only yesterday the government of Milton Obote of Uganda was toppled by its own army! There are two conditions necessary for peace in a nation.

i. Obedience to God's Word

Isaiah says that if a nation obeys God's commandments, the consequences will be abundant peace which leads to many more blessings, hence we read: 'O that you had hearkened to my commandments; then your peace would have been like a river, and your righteousness like the waves of the sea' (Isa. 48:18).

ii. Establishment of Justice and Righteousness

Again Isaiah says: 'Then justice will dwell in the wilderness and righteousness abide in the fruitful field. And the effect of righteousness will be quietness and trust for ever' (Isa. 32:16–17).

Creating the Conditions for Peace

Justice and righteousness as conditions for peace are central themes in the ministry of the prophets. The false prophets were saying 'peace, peace' when conditions for peace were not being fulfilled. Analysing what he saw, Jeremiah says: 'Everyone was greedy for unjust gain; they were stubbornly rebellious. All acted corruptly (Jer. 6:13, 28).

Justice and righteousness are the keys to peace in Kenya. Justice shields and defends peace. We need peace in the Church, and the Church must in turn demonstrate God's peace by exercising justice in all its activities, such as in the way we choose our own leaders.

We need peace in our schools, at the university and in all other institutions of higher learning. We need industrial peace that is guaranteed by just wages for work done. We need peace in our homes which is guaranteed by just relationships between husband, wife and children. Likewise we must establish justice in ensuring fair distribution of our resources and in our concern for the welfare of the poor, the hungry and the powerless. We must be good stewards of the soil and use it to increase food production so that we do not have to depend on *Gathirikari* (yellow maize supplied by the government as relief food) during famine, e.g. 1984.

We need peace in the Kenyan politics, by (among other things), holding fair grassroot party elections. We were impressed with the effort made to encourage people to join Kanu and to take part in the recently concluded party elections. We congratulate all those who were elected to posts in a just and fair manner. But there are places not only here in Kirinyaga but probably also in some other parts of the country where much was wrong. Justice even in party elections must not only be done but must also be seen to have been done.

The grassroot elections in which people lined up to vote enabled Wananchi to see and to judge for themselves whether there was justice or none at all. By and large justice was done; but those pockets of injustice may have given some people leadership without the authority of the people. It is possible to have power without authority. That is not justice, and it is not the way of peace.

I say these things because I love the Church and I love Kirinyaga. I say that because I have deep affection for our political leaders, whatever grouping they belong to. I say that because I love peace and I want to pursue it.

The way of peace is obedience to God, righteousness and justice. Many civil servants and Church leaders would have liked to participate in the elections, but their public positions and conscience forbid them to identify themselves publicly with individual groupings. It is my hope and prayer that future elections will be conducted by secret ballot.

The elections are now over. The challenge to the newly elected leaders is to work for what really matters in the life of the nation. I urge them to work for peace and unity by loving even those they consider to be enemies. 'Struggle for reconciliation and work for justice and righteousness. That is the way of peace, that is the *Nyayo philosophy* as I understand it.'

Pursuance of True Peace

In calling us to the way of peace, Paul tells us to focus our minds on eight qualities:

> Whatever is true, whatever is honourable;
> Whatever is just, whatever is pure;
> Whatever is lovely, whatever is gracious;
> Whatever is excellent, whatever is worthy of praise.

These are the qualities that all Christians should now aim at as we look forward to the next ten years of the Diocese. In the past decade, I have laboured day and night, to lead this diocese in the way of peace. I have spared no energy. Yet many times I have stumbled, and I ask for God's forgiveness where I have had shortcomings, and where I have failed to prophesy.

Jesus said, 'I pray for those who will believe in me through their message, that all of them may be one Father, just as you are in me and I am in you, may they also be united so that the world may believe that you have sent me (Jn. 17:20). Amen.

After the service, all the leaders present were invited for luncheon at Kirinyaga Technical Institute near Kutus. The luncheon was conspicuously boycotted by supporters of James Njiru and G.K. Kariithi who had won the recently concluded party elections. Mr John Matere Keriri and Mr Nahashon Njuno came for the luncheon and thanked the Bishop for his sermon.

A few days later a delegation of eight supporters of G.K. Kariithi came to see the Bishop at his office in Embu to complain about the sermon. The complaint was mainly that the Bishop had said that Mr G.K. Kariithi and his followers were elected as Kanu leaders in Gichugu constituency by vote rigging. The Bishop read the manuscript of his sermon which clearly stated that, 'by and large justice was done: but those pockets of injustice may have given some people leadership without the authority of the people'.

Three years later, Mr G.K. Kariithi was deposed from Kanu chairmanship in Gichugu because of rigged party elections won by Nahashon Njuno who had by now joined the camp of James Njiru. The Bishop was the only person who publicly protested against the rigging of elections in favour of Nahashon Njuno.

7

Do Not be Conformed to This World

Romans 12:1–2

A sermon preached at St Paul's Pro-Cathedral Embu on 27th July 1986

THE SETTING

Until 1986, the Voice of Kenya (VOK) had a regular programme of broadcast services from a variety of Churches around the country. Among other benefits, these broadcast services gave Christian leaders a chance to address the whole nation and to preach a message that would uplift, teach or challenge the hearers. By the time this sermon appeared, VOK's policy was already under review and so it was only a much edited version that was heard. But soon after, VOK dropped the live broadcast programme altogether.

VOK's sensitivity at that time cannot be clearly explained because there didn't seem to be any significant crisis in Church and State relations. After all the Church was backing the government in rejecting the subversive activities of Mwakenya, an underground political organization. In international affairs, the government had shown its abhorrence of apartheid by withdrawing the Kenyan team from the Commonwealth Games in Edinburgh. At some personal cost and inconvenience, the Bishop had supported this stand by withdrawing from his post as official chaplain to the Games.

Nevertheless one issue in the world of politics was causing concern at this time. Certain musicians had begun to take Christian hymns and choruses, and after adapting the words slightly had used these songs in praise of certain leaders in Kenya. In common with many other Christians, the Bishop found this unacceptable.

THE SERMON

I appeal to you therefore, brethren, by the mercies of God, to present your bodies as a living sacrifice, holy and acceptable to God, which is your spiritual worship. Do not be conformed to this world but be transformed by the renewal of your mind,

> that you may prove what is the will of God, what is good and acceptable and perfect [Rom. 12:1–2].

In these two verses, Paul makes three appeals to the Christians. In this broadcast service, I would like us carefully to examine these three appeals that St Paul, speaking from the depth of his heart, presents to us.

1. Present Your Bodies as a Living Sacrifice

To the first hearers of this message, this was a most revolutionary challenge. Paul lived in a world dominated by Greek culture. The Greeks could not have talked of a human being presenting his body to God, because to them, what mattered was not the body but the soul. Indeed, the body was considered to be but a shell and a prison house of the soul. The Greek gnostics believed that the soul of a person comes from God, and that the physical body which now imprisons the soul was the work of demonic and evil powers. The body should therefore be despised and punished. The Christian, by contrast, believes that his body as well as his soul were created by God and therefore belong to God. The Christian can therefore serve God just as well with his body as his spirit; indeed his body is the temple of the Holy Spirit, the place in which the Holy Spirit dwells, the instrument through which the Holy Spirit works. The fact that the Son of God came to the world by incarnation, that is, by taking a human body, means that God himself did not despise the human body. The Son of God took it, he lived in it and wished to glorify God in it.

So in the Greek world which despised the human body, St Paul had the courage to urge Christians to offer their bodies as a living sacrifice, holy and acceptable to God. What St Paul is telling you and me is something like this: My brother, my sister – take your body, the tasks you carry out every day, in the kitchen, at your shop, in your company or factory, in your farm, in the government office, in the county council or in Parliament. Offer all this as an act of worship to God.

In the Bible, the word worship is always used in reference to service to and reverence for God. When Paul says that this presentation of our bodies is 'spiritual worship', he tells us that the true worship, the real and genuine spiritual worship is the offering of one's body, and of all that one does every day to God. William Barclay says that real worship is not the offering of elaborate prayers and elaborate liturgy in a Church. Real worship is something which sees the whole world as the temple of the living God, and every common deed as an act of worship. Seen in this way, our coming to Church to worship becomes the climax of the daily offering of our bodies as a living sacrifice, holy and acceptable to God. This is also what the prophet Micah meant when he found that the people of Israel had the wrong concept of worship. He said:

> What shall I bring to the Lord, the God of heaven, when I come to worship him? Will the Lord be pleased if I bring him thousands of sheep, or endless streams of olive oil? Shall I offer him my first born child to pay for my sins? No, the Lord has told us what is good. What he requires is this: To do what is just, show constant love, and humbly obey your God [Mic. 6:6–7].

This shows us that the act of offering our bodies means doing what is just in our dealings with other people. It is to show constant love to mankind, and humbly to obey God.

A driver whose *Matatu* (public vehicle) or bus is not road worthy and who packs his passengers like bags of potatoes is not offering his body and his career as a living sacrifice, holy and acceptable to God. The *Miraa* (*Khat*) vehicle driver, who drives along the new Meru–Embu road at terrifying speed, even through the narrow main street of Runyenjes town, is not offering his body as a living sacrifice to God.

While you are right to say, 'I am going to Church to worship God', you can also say, 'I am going to the factory, to the shop, to the office, to school, to the farm to worship God' – as long as these three elements are found in what you are going to do there: that you are going to do what is just to your employer or your customers, and others that you encounter at work; that you will show love and consideration to all those who you encounter throughout the day; that you will humbly obey God. This is an act of worship! This concept of worship demands a radical change. This brings us to Paul's next appeal.

2. Do Not be Conformed to this World

The Greek word which has been translated 'conformed' has the connotation of a potter who takes clay and moulds it into whatever shape he likes. He can take clay and make the shape of a plate, or a cup, or a pot. Hence Paul is telling Christians not to be moulded into whatever shape the world wishes to mould them. The appeal is, 'Do not try to match your life to all the fashions of the world; do not be like a chameleon which takes its colour from its surroundings.'

Indeed, Paul is telling us not to let the world decide what we are going to do. St Paul clearly appeals to the Christians of Rome, indeed he commands them not to let the world or the age in which they were living decide what they were going to do, as they set out each day to perform the ordinary duties of life.

There was, of course, the world of the politics of the Roman Empire; and there was the world of its sophisticated Greek culture. In the political world, the government supported Emperor worship: in fact, Caesar Augustus, who had brought peace to the Mediterranean world, was hailed as the incarnation of divinity. Statues of Augustus were erected in various cities, and religious ceremonies were instituted for him. Every person living in the Roman Empire was expected to shout, 'Caesar is Lord!' To consider anyone else to be Lord was tantamount to being seditious. To be a loyal citizen in those days meant worshipping the Emperor and being ready to declare that Caesar is Lord.

It was in such a political climate that Paul had the courage to tell the Christians in Rome: 'Do not be conformed to the world. Do not let the world decide for you what to say and what to do. If the world around you is worshipping Caesar, they are worshipping an idol. Refuse to worship him even if they say you have become anti-Caesar. If they are saying, "Caesar is Lord", tell them "Jesus Christ is Lord". Do not praise Caesar with any songs which should be reserved only for Jesus Christ our Lord. If you hear the world around you sing such songs, refuse to sing them, for a Christian must give all praise, worship and thanksgiving to God.'

But of course Paul was not unrealistic. He recognized the place of the Emperor, and in the next chapter he made yet another appeal to Christians.

> Let everyone be subject to the governing authorities. For there is no authority except from God, and those that exist have been instituted by Gŏd. Therefore he who resists the authorities resists what God has appointed, and those who resist will incur judgement [Rom. 13:1–2].

Yet Paul does not tell Christians to accept the authority of those in power unconditionally: their authority is acceptable as long as rulers are not a terror to good conduct, as long as they do not demand to be worshipped, which is tantamount to usurping that which is the sole prerogative of God who has appointed them. The Christian must not allow the political climate to mould him into its own shape. The Christian must not allow the popular prevailing culture and fashion to dictate to him what to do and what to say.

We can identify some of the implications of this radical demand to us in our contemporary Kenya.

It means that the Christian civil servant will refuse bribes even if he finds that accepting bribes is a common practice among his colleagues. To accept bribes would be tantamount to being moulded to fit the world around him.

The Christian shopkeeper will not use faulty weights and measures, nor will he hoard goods or increase prices of scarce commodities unfairly.

A Christian member of a district Kanu branch will be the first to resist indiscriminate expulsions of other politicians from the party, simply because they have a different point of view. When we have only one party, the party must be prepared to accept differing points of view.

A Christian soldier in military service must have complete allegiance to the President and to the country, and must not be a party to any attempt to overthrow a democratically-elected government by the use of the power of the gun.

A Christian, wherever he might be, who comes across underground subversive activities such as Mwakenya, will refuse to be moulded into the shape of Mwakenya.

A Christian who feels concerned about issues affecting any section of society will openly express his views. This is why CPK bishops have openly expressed their solidarity with Bishop Alexander Muge and the Christians of the Diocese of Eldoret who are being unfairly attacked by politicians.

The writer of the Book of Wisdom says, 'Someone who holds back the truth causes trouble, but the one who openly criticizes works for peace' (Prob. 19:10). The Christian man or woman, wherever he or she might be, will refuse to be moulded into the shape of the world around. Wherever such a person finds unfairness or unjust structures, they must be prepared to stand and be counted in rejecting those evils. They will give to Caesar what is Caesar's, but will refuse to give Caesar that which can be given only to God. But for the Christian to have the courage to take such a stand, he must be willing to accept St Paul's third and final appeal in this passage.

3. Be Transformed, by the Renewal of Your Mind

The Christian must not live in the old fashion, responding to the will of the lower nature; instead he must be metamorphozed by the renewal of his mind in submission to the lordship of Jesus Christ and by allowing the power of the Holy Spirit to operate in his life. This is the only way he can prove what is the will of God, what is good and acceptable and perfect.

One of the greatest urges of our spiritual lives is to know God's will, especially when it comes to major decisions in life. Recently, I found myself confronted by a major problem requiring me to make an important decision. About two years ago I was invited by the Christian Churches of the city of Edinburgh in Scotland, to be one of the two Chaplains to the Commonwealth Games. I accepted the invitation and started preparing myself for participation at the games. About two weeks ago I bought the ticket and on the 12th July I left Kenya for East Germany and Edinburgh. While in East Germany it was made clear to me that the government of Kenya had decided to withdraw from participating in the Games. I found myself in a great dilemma as to whether I should go to Scotland to minister to the athletes or not.

I did not want to conform to what the world was saying. First and foremost I wanted to do what was God's will for me in the circumstances. I cannot claim that a voice came from heaven to tell me to boycott the Games. But it was clear to me that apartheid is an evil system of government, and it is within God's will that it should be dismantled. Hence, the pressure that the government of Kenya and those of many other countries are putting on Britain and other great powers to impose sanctions on South Africa may be one way in which God's will for South Africa can be fulfilled. If therefore my participation in the Games would be understood as giving my blessing to Margaret Thatcher and her government to continue supporting apartheid, then I would be acting contrary to the will of God for South Africa. Consequently, I had to cancel my journey to Edinburgh despite the fact that for a period of two years I had been looking forward with great expectation to participate in the Games.

St Paul has given us a guideline on how we can know God's will: we are not to be conformed to this world; we are not to let the world decide for us what we are going to do; and, we must be transformed by the renewal of our minds – a kind of a metamorphosis. The tadpole cannot know anything about the dry land unless it undergoes a metamorphosis and becomes a frog, able to jump out of the water and breathe in the air. We too must be metamorphozed in our thoughts.

God is always willing to reveal his will to all men and women including yourself, as long as you are willing to tune your mind to the wavelength of heaven. The BBC broadcasts to the whole world 24 hours a day: but only the person who switches on his radio and tunes to the wavelength of the BBC is able to hear it. The same is true with God. He is always speaking: but those who hear him are only those who wish to know his will; what is good, acceptable and perfect. They will have their minds transformed and renewed as they are tuned to the wavelength of heaven.

In the name of the Father, and of the Son, and of the Holy Spirit. Amen.

8

Cain Strikes Again

A sermon preached at Getuya in Kirinyaga on 17th December 1987 at the funeral service of Mr Mwai Karani, a Mombasa businessman and politician, who was killed in Port Reitz, Mombasa

THE SETTING

In December 1987 Kenyans were shocked by the murder of a prominent local businessman and politician, Mr Mwai Karani, at his Port Reitz home in the coastal town of Mombasa. A son of a Church elder from Kirinyaga, Karani was brought home to be buried, and the Bishop was invited to conduct the funeral service and to preach. Among those who attended were all the members of Parliament from Mombasa led by the Hon Shariff Nassir; local politicians, Mr James Njiru, the chairman of Kanu in Kirinyaga District, Hon John M. Keriri and Hon Nahashon Njuno and other prominent leaders. Mrs Njeri Karani, a murder suspect, was escorted by police to the funeral.

Before the service started, there was an attempt by the D.O. Ndia Division and the Chief of the area to exclude Hon John M. Keriri the MP of the area from addressing the gathering. Indeed the D.O. wanted to be the master of ceremonies just to ensure that the MP did not speak. The Bishop told the D.O. 'Once I put on my robes, you will realize who the master of ceremonies is. This is an Anglican burial service and the Bishop is in charge from beginning to end.' In his sermon, the Bishop preached strongly against the evil of murder, whether for political motives or for any other reason. He was sure that among those standing there were some who knew how Karani had met his death and so this sermon served as both a rebuke and a challenge to them. In fact, as it emerged, Karani's murder was not political. Nevertheless the challenge remains (for both politicians and all the other people), to avoid the mistake of Cain and instead to become 'my brother's keeper', as God intends.

THE SERMON

Cain said to his brother Abel, 'Let us go out to the field', and when they were in the field, Cain rose up against his brother Abel and killed him. Then the Lord said to

> Cain, 'Where is Abel your brother?' He said, 'I do not know; Am I my brother's keeper?' And the Lord said 'What have you done? The voice of your brother's blood is crying to me from the ground. And now you are cursed from the ground which has opened its mouth to receive your brother's blood from your hand.'

1. Introduction

In the Book of Genesis 4:1–15 we have a record of the first murder in Biblical history. In this sad story we have three characters: Cain, Abel and God.

Cain was the firstborn child of our original parents Adam and Eve. Cain chose to be a farmer, and Abel his younger brother chose to be a shepherd. The Bible records that after some time, Cain brought some of his harvest and gave it as an offering to the Lord. Then Abel brought the first lamb born to one of his sheep, killed it and gave the best parts of it as an offering. The Lord was pleased with Abel and his offering. This was probably because Abel gave his offering in faith and with a pure motive, whereas Cain made his offering for self-glory and not by faith.

God refused to accept Cain's offering because he was an unrepentant evil man. God will accept the offerings of sinful men only if there is true and sincere repentance as the prophet Isaiah said concerning Jerusalem:

> Jerusalem, your rulers and your people are like those of Sodom and Gomorrah. Listen to what the Lord is saying to you. Pay attention to what our God is teaching you. He says, 'Do you think I want all these sacrifices you keep offering me? I have had more than enough of the sheep you burn as sacrifices and of the fat of your animals. I am tired of the blood of bulls and sheep and goats. Who asked you to do all this tramping about in my temple? It was useless to bring your offerings. I am disgusted with the smell of incense you burn. I cannot stand your new moon festivals, your Sabbath and your religious gatherings; they are all corrupted by your sins . . . When you lift your hands in prayer, I will not look at you. No matter how much you pray, I will not listen, for your hands are covered with blood. Wash yourselves clean. Stop all this evil and learn to do right. See that justice is done – help those who are oppressed, give orphans their right, and defend the widows' [Isa. 1:10–17].

2. Cain Murders Abel

God accepted Abel's offering because he was careful in offering the very best part of his sacrifice. Instead of repenting Cain became furious when his offering was rejected. Then God posed this question to him, 'Why are you angry? Why that scowl on your face? If you had done the right thing you could be smiling; but because you have done evil, sin is crouching at your door. It wants to rule you, but you must overcome it' (4:6–7).

God tried to persuade Cain to repent but instead of repenting he continued with his evil intentions. He persuaded his younger brother to go with him into the fields where he turned on him and killed him (4:8).

The first murder ever recorded in human history took place on that day. Cain killed Abel: the older and stronger brother killed his younger and more vulnerable brother. But why did Cain decide to kill his brother? There was only one motive: envy!

3. Envy: the Key Motive of Murder

To this day, envy continues to be the main motive for most of the murders committed in the world. When a person uses his brains and his hands and makes a fortune in business, not everyone is happy. Some may plot to eliminate him.

If a potential leader begins to show signs that he's likely to win an election, not everyone is happy. Envy creeps in and some start planning how he can be eliminated.

The *Cain* of jealousy and envy has struck again. That is why we have gathered here to witness the results of the wickedness of *Cain*. Mwai Karani, a capable Mombasa businessman, is in this coffin. Mwai Karani, a successful Kanu party official in his area of operation and a very promising politician, is lying here dead. The blood has been shed; *Cain* has struck once again!

4. Thou Shalt Not Murder

The sixth commandment says, 'Do not commit murder.' Why did God make this one of the ten commandments? It is because man is made in the image of God. Thus we read:

> Then God said, 'Let us make man in our image, after our likeness; and let them have dominion over the fish of the sea, and over the birds of the air, and over the cattle, and over all the earth.' So God created man in his own image, in the image of God he created him; male and female he created them [Gen. 1:26].

The fact that humanity is made in the image of God means that man has a special dignity above all other created things, and for that reason he should be respected and served, not exploited or eliminated. Murder is a most terrible crime, because it is the destruction of the very image of God. Because man is made in God's image, his life should be honoured. Only God who created man has the right to take his life, in accordance with his own will.

For a fellow human being to shed the blood of another is a serious sin, and a great offence to the Creator. Only under the very special circumstances permitted by God himself (for example, the capital punishment of a proven murderer) should human beings take the life of another human being. Otherwise, to shed another's blood and even to shed one's own blood by suicide, is a terrible sin. The Bible shows us that God is the author of human life, and he alone has the prerogative to take back that life if and when he so wishes.

5. Letting Be

From the beginning, the Bible describes God as a Creator. In the creation narrative of Genesis 1, God repeatedly says, 'Let there be . . .'; and in response to this command of God, the whole creation as we see it today sprang into existence.

God is the one who lets 'be', and the climax of his work of creation was to create human beings in his own image. When God created Adam and Eve, he commissioned them to continue with his task of creating. Man was created so that he can continue with God's creativity, and so that he too will learn to let 'be'.

The book *The Church in Response to Human Need* by Vinay Samuel and Chris Sugden has some good comments about human creativity.

When God made the earth, he could have finished it, but he didn't. He left it as a raw material – to tease us, and to tantalize us, to set us thinking, and experimenting, and risking, and adventuring. And therein we find our supreme interest in living. He gave us the challenge of raw materials: not the satisfaction of perfect, finished things. He left the music unsung and the drama unplayed.

He left the poetry undreamed, in order that men and women might not become bored, but engaged in stimulating, exciting, creative activities that keep them thinking, working, experimenting and experiencing all the joys and durable satisfaction of achievements.

Man was created so as to continue with God's creativity. He was created not to exploit his fellow human beings but to exploit the earth and rule over all created things. Abel was born into this world with the potential to be creative. He chose to look after sheep, which would in turn grow fat and multiply. But Cain killed him even before he had completed his task. Abel was born so as to realize his full potential of participating in and continuing with God's creativity. But Cain, his older and stronger brother, took away his life in its prime when he still had much energy and great plans for 'letting be'.

Here we have another reason why murder is a grievous sin. Like Abel, our brother Mwai Karani has been taken away from our midst before he had a chance to complete his work of using fully the gifts and talents which God gave him, that he might continue in creativity. His interest in politics is an indication that he was also interested in struggling for justice for his fellow human beings. To shed the blood of Mwai Karani is to cause a great loss, because he has been untimely stopped from co-operating with God in creating.

We have a duty to help every individual to realize his full potential in continuing with God's creation. It is a crime before God for anyone to try to hinder a fellow human being from 'letting be', that is from being creative, whether by committing murder or even by putting unnecessary obstacles in the path of his creative zeal.

If a person has the potential to be a businessman, our task is to help him to be successful in the use of his gifts. But Cain, with all his envy, will not let his brother use the gifts of his calling. There is no doubt that Mwai Karani had a talent for business. From simple beginnings, he had become a successful businessman in Mombasa. But he had not yet completed his task in this field, and Cain and his associates would not let him complete his task: they took away his life.

If a person feels he is called to be a leader and has gifts of leadership, we have a duty to help him to realize his full potential. If in the political world a person is duly elected to represent his community in the county council or in Parliament, our duty is not to hinder him but to assist him to succeed in his calling. Let the leaders be given every encouragement in their task of leadership. Those leaders who try to hinder other duly elected leaders in the performance of their duties, are guilty of hindering their fellow men, who are also made in the image of God. They are preventing those other leaders from continuing with God's creativity in the development of our nation.

Mwai Karani had demonstrated his leadership skills by being elected as an organizing secretary for the Mombasa West sub-branch of Kanu, and in vying for a parliamentary seat. But there are many Cains, and we can see the result of their evil work right here. Mwai Karani the organizing secretary lies dead.

Cain has stopped him from organizing Kanu in his sub-branch. His creativity in politics has been brought to a tragic end. He can no longer use his organizational gifts which God gave him. Cain has prevented his brother from being creative.

6. Where is Your Brother?

After Cain had killed Abel, God visited him and asked him, 'Where is your brother Abel?' 'I do not know,' Cain answered God. 'Am I my brother's keeper?' This is the second great question that God asked the first human beings. The first question was directed to Adam after he had eaten the forbidden fruit: 'Where are you, Adam?'

The sin of Adam seems to have opened the door for sin in the world. When God asked Cain, 'Where is your brother Abel?', then instead of seeing his sin and repenting, Cain continued to add more sin. He had already committed murder, and now he told a naked lie. But God told him, 'Why have you done this terrible thing? Your brother's blood is crying out to me from the ground, like a voice calling for revenge' (4:10).

This day, God is asking us, 'Where is your brother Mwai Karani?' And the people who know where he is – the people who murdered him in the early hours of 7th December at Port Reiz Corner, Changamwe, are the first people to tell God, 'We do not know where Mwai Karani is: are we our brother's keeper?' Yes, you are: your work was to protect your brother Mwai Karani and to help him realize his full potential, in business and in politics. Instead of protecting him, you have killed him and his blood is crying out to God from the ground, like a voice calling for revenge.

Although Mwai Karani is dead, his good work, though not completed, will continue to have an impact. But the murderers remain accused. Thus God pronounced judgement upon Cain, the first murderer in human history. 'You are placed under a curse and can no longer farm the soil. It has soaked up your brother's blood as if it had opened its mouth to receive it when you killed him. If you try to grow crops, the soil will not produce anything. You will be a homeless wanderer on the earth' (4.11–12).

But God is also a merciful God, for he can even forgive a murderer if he truly repents. Thus the prophet Isaiah is bold to say,

> The Lord says, 'Now let us settle the matter. You are stained red with sin, but I will wash you as clean as snow. Although your stains are deep red, you will be as white as wool. If you will only obey me, you will eat the good things the land produces. But if you defy me, you are doomed to die. I, the Lord, have spoken' [Isa. 1:18–20].

7. Justice be Our Shield and Defender

Our National anthem begins with a prayer to God: *O God of all creation. Bless this our land and nation.* God does not give his blessings in a vacuum. He brings his blessings where there is justice, peace, love and unity. Our country will be blessed if we allow justice to be our shield and defender.

This is not the first time that our country has experienced the murder of a politician. Shortly after independence, Gama Pinto was shot dead at his Nairobi house. In July 1969, Tom Mboya, one of the most talented politicians this country has ever known, was shot dead in a Nairobi street. About five years later, in March 1975, Josiah Mwangi Kariuki was murdered in the Ngong Hills. About five years later, Owiti, the Member of Parliament from Siaya, was also murdered. Today another politician lies here dead. Cain, in his striking missions has struck yet again!

In each one of these murder cases, we were told that no stone would be left unturned until the murderers were found and dealt with appropriately. Indeed, the government of the day did its best to trace the murderers of these great sons of Kenya. Nevertheless the murderers of Hon J.M. Kariuki remain at large. It may be that some stones were too heavy to be lifed, and as a result to this day we have never officially been told who murdered 'J.M.' Justice neither defended nor shielded J.M. Kariuki.

We hope this will not be the case with the murderers of Mwai Karani, whose blood is crying out to God from the ground, like a voice calling for revenge. May God frustate the plans of any other children of Cain who might be planning to take the life of yet another political leader. We do not want this country to be soaked with the blood of any more innocent people.

Likewise may God frustrate those who plan to murder anyone created in the image of God, whoever he might be. May God restrain Cain and bind him, so that he does not repeat his work in this our beloved country. And may we all, never, ever be associated in any way with those who plan to shed the blood of their brothers.

May we truly become our brother's keeper, protecting him, and even exposing the plans of the clan of Cain. May our leaders be daily protected from the hands of murderers so that they can fulfil their task of leadership, and may the strong hand of our government defend and shield all citizens from the evil works of Cain and his associates. In this way, God will answer our daily prayer, 'Bless this our land and nation.' Amen.

AFTERMATH OF THE SERMON

Two days after this Sermon I went to Mombasa and I met Hon Shariff Nassir in a hotel and I introduced myself to him. He was very excited to meet me. He told me that he was not aware that the preacher was Bishop David Gitari. But when I said, 'Some stones are too heavy to be lifted' he asked the person sitting next to him the name of the preacher. He then told me that had he known Bishop Gitari was present at the funeral he would have completely changed the text of his speech. He then called a friend and introduced him to me saying, 'This is Bishop Gitari, one of the most courageous Bishops in this country who always speaks the truth. But as politicians it is our duty to attack him even when we know what he is saying is true.' He then concluded by saying, 'Bishop, continue speaking the truth even when we (politicians attack) you.'

9

Shattered Dreams, Realized Hopes

Sermon preached at St Thomas' Church Kerugoya on Sunday, 10th April 1988

THE SETTING

The February and March 1988 countrywide elections were held for both the local councils and the National Assembly. The voting was held in two rounds. The first one in February was for the nomination of candidates for the ruling party, Kanu. The voting was conducted for the first time by queuing. Any candidate who secured 70% or more of this poll became the sole candidate and was automatically elected. Candidates with less than 30% of votes were eliminated. The General Election proper came in March, for those constituencies where more than one candidate was nominated. This one was done through secret ballot.

Unfortunately in many parts of the country, there was evidence of massive vote rigging and intimidation, which reduced the confidence of voters in the outcome of the elections. Some of the evidence was published in Beyond *magazine. Despite the intercession of internationally-respected figures such as former President Jimmy Carter,* Beyond *magazine was banned by the government.*

In some constituencies where there was clear evidence of blatant rigging of elections, a repeat of elections was allowed, yet in other similar cases, a repeat was rejected. We had evidence that in all the three Kirinyaga constituencies, elections were rigged. However, there is no use crying over spilt milk. Whether or not we approved of the manner in which some leaders were selected, we had to accept that they were in fact now in power. The Bishop felt obliged to encourage the Christians to support the (s)elected leaders and further to urge the disappointed losers to take heart and not allow themselves to be overwhelmed with frustration. But at the same time the Christian leader has a duty to tell the truth and in this case the Bishop, who had very much been involved in monitoring the elections (and as such knew the whole truth) could not keep the truth from the people: and the truth was that Elections in Kirinyaga were massively rigged. You might have heard the Bishop on many occasions alluding to new political mathematics in which a man with only five voters behind him is declared winner and his other contestant who has five hundred voters behind him is declared the loser. All that took place in 1988.

In the following sermon the Bishop addresses the frustration factor and further offers hope. The Sermon was delivered during a special Diocesan service organized specifically to pray for the newly (s)elected leaders. Significantly, this was the first such service in the Diocese in which all the M.P.s failed to turn up. (See also Chapter Two of this book for another sermon on Shattered Dreams.)

THE SERMON

1. A Dream of Life

One of St Paul's greatest dreams was to preach the gospel in Spain. He said this very clearly when he wrote to the Roman Christians concerning his future plans:

> But now I have finished my work in these regions and since I have been wanting for so many years to come and see you, I hope to do so now. I would like to see you on my way to Spain, and be helped by you to go there, after I have enjoyed visiting you for a while. [Rom. 15:22–24]

St Paul's plan after he had preached the gospel from Jerusalem all the way to what is now called Yugoslavia was to continue with his missionary work until he reached Spain. There is no doubt that preaching the gospel in Spain had become his greatest ambition. A number of reasons made Paul want to go to Spain:

a. He wanted to obey our Lord's commission to his disciples to preach the gospel not only in Jerusalem, Judea and Samaria but to the uttermost parts of the earth. Paul may have thought that Spain and Portugal were the uttermost parts of the world, as they were on the shores of the Atlantic Ocean and the American continent had not as yet been discovered.

b. St Paul says, 'My ambition has always been to proclaim the good news in places where Christ has not been heard of so as not to build on a foundation laid by someone else' (Rom. 15:20). Since someone else had already preached the gospel in Rome, Paul did not want to settle in Rome: he wanted to move on to Spain, where nobody had as yet gone to do missionary work.

c. Again, at this period in the history of the Roman Empire, some of the best educated men were Spaniards. Men like Seneca, Quintillian and others were among the top intellectuals in the Empire. St Paul, the most learned of all the apostles, was telling himself, 'If only I can reach Spain, then I can touch some of these top intellectuals and win them for Christ. Then they, in turn, will help to turn the world upside down for Christ.'

2. The Dream is Shattered

Though Paul's greatest dream was to reach Spain, his dream was never fulfilled. He went to Jerusalem to take some famine relief to the brethren there. While he was there, he was arrested inside the Temple for allegedly behaving 'in a manner likely to cause a breach of peace', and could easily have been killed. The allegation was that he had defiled the temple by entering it with a gentile called Trophimus from Ephesus. The allegation was not true. Nevertheless a mob attacked him and he was rescued by Roman soldiers, and detained for two years at Caesarea by the sea. After two years he appealed to the Emperor and he was taken to Rome in chains and kept in detention while awaiting trial. And so, instead of going to Spain, St Paul ended up in a Roman jail. His dream of ever reaching Spain was completely shattered.

Each one of us has an ambition in life: we have our own dreams of reaching our desired Spain. How do you react in the circumstances of a shattered dream? Think of a girl who falls in love with a handsome young man, and her greatest dream is to be married to that boy. Marriage to that particular man becomes her Spain. Supposing the man changes his mind? The same may happen to a man who is jilted by his girlfriend. The experience is usually extremely shattering.

You may get married quite happily, but then your dream of having children becomes just a distant Spain. After seven years of marriage, you find that you have no child. Having a child becomes an unattainable dream. How do you react? Or probably you have children but they are all of one gender, and if you are an African man, you cannot sleep well until the day your wife will bear you a son. And so you have six daughters and you are frantically hoping that the next one is going to be a son. Then it turns out to be another baby girl! How do you react? Do you become shattered to the point of gouging out your wife's eyes in the way one Mr Kaguai of Kiaga village in Kirinyaga District did to his wife Piah Njoki?

You may be dreaming that your own children will follow after you and make great achivements in life; yet all these dreams turn out to be mere distant Spain.

Your dream, your distant Spain, might be that you want to be promoted: a teacher dreams that he might become a headmaster, an assistant chief wants to become a chief, a D.O. wants to become a D.C., and the D.C. of course would like to become a P.C. A priest would not hate becoming a rural dean and an archdeacon might be quietly hoping to become a bishop one day! How do you react when others get the positions you were eyeing?

Your life's dream may be a deep desire to serve this nation as an elected councillor or as a Member of Parliament. Your Spain is to reach *Bunge* (parliament): you campaigned as hard as you could, spent a lot of money, only to find that in the end someone else has overtaken you in the race. How do you react? Or you may be lucky enough to be elected, only to find that you are not appointed to a position in government which you had hoped to have as the Spain of your dream. How do you react?

3. The Frustration of Shattered Dreams

One common reaction to shattered dreams is a sense of disappointment. A disappointed person is first and foremost a blamer: one who tends to complain always and to blame others for his failures. Life becomes nothing but complaints. He loses interest in life, and cannot enjoy even the most beautiful music. He consequently withdraws into himself and refuses to open his heart to anyone. He becomes an introvert. Sometimes these people become psychiatric cases. Finally, they lose interest in life so much that they even find fault with God. Paul could easily have complained to Jesus: 'You appointed me to be an apostle to the Gentiles; but see now my time is just wasted in a Roman jail.' But he did not complain.

4. Turning a Liability into an Asset

> I want you to know, my brothers, that the things that have happened to me have really helped the progress of the gospel. As a result, the whole palace guard and all the others here know that I am in prison because I am a servant of Christ. And my being in prison has given most of the brothers more confidence in the Lord, so that they grow bolder all the time to preach the message fearlessly [Philp. 1:12–14]

Instead of complaining Paul turned his liability to an asset. Thus he could say: *I want you to know, my brothers, that the things that have happened to me have really helped the progress of the gospel . . .*

Instead of preaching the gospel in Spain, Paul was given a unique opportunity of proclaiming the gospel in the corridors of the Roman power; preaching even to the palace guard (the emperor's own soldiers). Thank God that St Paul never went to Spain: for when could those soldiers, from the most influential unit in the Empire, have heard the gospel had St Paul not been taken to that prison cell? What appeared to be a liability now became a great asset for the extension of God's kingdom.

5. Encouraging Others

St Paul was also able to give encouragement and confidence to all the Christians who came to visit him. In that prison cell he was allowed to be visited by many Christian friends. He was able to give them encouragement to stand firm despite the many trials which he, and they, faced.

6. Managing Time Well

Paul refused to be an idle prisoner. He called his scribe and he dictated letters of great importance which were sent to various Churches. It was in prison that St Paul wrote the letters to the Ephesians, Philippians, Colossians, Timothy, Titus and to Philemon. These letters are among the best epistles inherited by the Church throughout history. It is amazing to think that they were written by a prisoner in a Roman jail, who had refused to be conquered by the failure to realize his dream of going to Spain. If Paul had gone to Spain, he would not have had an opportunity of writing those great letters. To this day, we find encouragement as we read the words written in prison almost 2000 years ago:

> Rejoice in the Lord always, and again I say Rejoice. Let all men know your forebearance, the Lord is at hand. Have no anxiety about anything, but in everything by prayer and supplication with thanksgiving let your requests be made known to God. And the peace of God which passes all understanding, shall keep your hearts and your minds in Christ Jesus [Philp. 4:4–7].

Have you gone through a period in which your desire to reach the Spain of your dreams has not been fulfilled? Has this been a shattering experience?

The Christian gospel does not allow us to become despondent and to lose the zest for living. It encourages us to confront our problems so that we do not allow the problems to conquer us, but rather we conquer them. We have to change what now appears to be a liability into an asset.

7. Realized Dream: The Case of Queen Esther

Not everyone has had a shattering experience: indeed, there are many who have reached the Spain of their dreams. However, if you had a dream of reaching a position of influence, and now you have reached that position, then remember the experience of Esther, who became the Queen of the Persian Empire. Her story is told in chapter four of the book called by her name. But in brief, Esther was a Jewess who was selected to be Queen after a series of beauty contests in every province of the Persian Empire but the King did not know that she was a Jewess. When Haman the Prime Minister bribed the king into agreeing that the Jewish population should be extinguished, it was Queen Esther who spoke to the King and Haman's evil plotting was brought to nought. But in the whole process, Mordecai's heated letter to Esther was of maximum significance:

> Esther, do not imagine you are safer than any of the other Jews in the Empire. If you keep quiet at a time like this, help will come to the Jews in some other way and they will be saved. But you will die and your father's family will come to an end. Yet who knows, may be it was for a time like this that you were made a Queen [Est. 4:13–14].

To you, men and women who are occupying influential positions: you are in those positions so as to play a part in preserving peace and tranquillity in our nation. It is for a time like this that you are where God has placed you. Only do not keep quiet in the face of injustices, or when you can say something that might avert a crisis – see that justice is done without fear or favour. It is not our wish to experience what Habakkuk experienced in the 7th century BC — the things that made him open his book with a complaint to God:

> O Lord, how long must I call for help before you listen, before you save us from violence? Why do you make me see such trouble. How can you endure to look on such wrongdoing. Destruction and violence are all around me, and there is fighting and quarrelling everywhere. The evil men get the better of the righteous, and so justice is perverted. [Hab. 1:2–4].

God has put you in an influential position at this time so that you can vigilantly struggle for justice and peace. Only, do not keep quiet when you should speak to avert injustices. Ensure that no one is punished simply because he stood in the 'wrong' line during the queueing.

8. Respect for Leaders

> We beg you, brothers, to pay proper respect to those who work among you, who guide and instruct you in the Christian life. Treat them with the greatest respect and love because of the work they do. Be at peace among yourselves [1 Thes. 5:6].

It is the duty of those who are led to respect the leaders and all in positions of leadership. It is God who gives permission for there to be men and women in authority because he desires orderly living. We must respect our councillors and our parliamentarians not necessarily because of who they are but primarily because of the offices they hold, and the work they do for us. We must therefore give the greatest respect to all the newly elected councillors, our new members of parliament and those appointed to serve this nation as ministers in various ministries. The majority of them have been elected in rigged elections. Nevertheless they have been sworn in as leaders. We shall continue reminding them that they have gained power without authority of the electorate. Despite this, let us give them a chance. We shall however continue praying for the end of the rigging of elections.

Above all, we must show the greatest respect and honour to our beloved President and we should constantly pray for him, as St Paul ordered in his first letter to Timothy:

> I urge petitions, prayers, requests and thanksgiving to be offered to God for all people: for kings and all others who are in authority, that we may live a quiet life with proper conduct. This is good and it pleases God our saviour who wants everyone to be saved and to come to know the truth [1 Tim. 2:1–4].

We must not rush to condemn leaders even when they make mistakes. We could make mistakes if we were in the same positions. They work under great pressure, and we should pray for them that God may help them to make the right decisions at the right time.

I wish to conclude with Paul's (concluding) words in his first letter to the Thessalonians:

> We urge you, our brothers, to warn the idle, encourage the timid, help the weak, be patient with everyone. See that no one pays back wrong for wrong, but at all times make it your aim to do good to one another and to all people. Be joyful always, pray at all times, be thankful in all circumstances. This is what God wants from you in your life in union with Christ Jesus. Do not restrain the Holy Spirit, do not despise inspired messages. Put all things to the test; keep what is good, and avoid every kind of evil. May the God who gives us peace make you holy in every way, and keep your whole being – spirit, soul and body – free from every fault at the coming of our Lord Jesus Christ. He who calls you will do it because he is faithful . . . [1 Thess. 5:14–28].

The grace of our Lord Jesus Christ be with you. Amen.

10

Render To Caesar . . .

A sermon preached at St Paul's Cathedral Embu on Sunday 9th October 1988 during the Annual Mothers' Union Rally of the Diocese of Mt Kenya East

THE SETTING

On 19th September 1988 the ruling party, Kanu held its grassroots elections, which culminated in a national delegates' conference held at the Nyayo Stadium Nairobi on September 24th and attended by 3600 delegates. The delegates' conference selected officers for national Kanu posts, and also passed twelve resolutions on a variety of subjects, some of which were highly contentious. One such resolution praised the role of civil servants in conducting the grassroots elections even when Kenyans knew that the said elections had been massively rigged. Another resolution called for the government to 'reassess' its relations with the National Council of Churches of Kenya (NCCK), and made unsubstantiated allegations that NCCK did not support the government.

These resolutions were read out to delegates by the newly elected General Secretary of Kanu, Mr Moses Mudavadi, who had just arrived from overseas where he had gone for medical treatment. A motion adopting the resolutions en bloc was then proposed and accepted with no debate whatsoever. When the Bishop learned of this procedure, he issued a press statement urging that future delegates' conferences should be allowed to debate contentious resolutions before passing them, otherwise delegates will appear to be used as mere rubber stamps of resolutions that have been drafted by a few people. As usual there was an angry outcry from politicians in reaction to the Bishop's remarks.

On 29th September, Parliament suspended its ordinary business for two and a half hours in order to hold an emergency debate 'to condemn Bishop Gitari'. Speaker after speaker rose to accuse him of being subversive while others said that the Bishop is in the payroll of foreign masters.

The then Vice President Mr Josphat Karanja was almost the only one who tried to respond to the real issue raised by the Bishop, when he termed Kanu as a club with its own rules. Interestingly enough, six months later Dr Karanja was dismissed from office after a debate on his conduct, to which he was not allowed to contribute!

It was in this overheated atmosphere that the Bishop preached a sermon clarifying the relationship between the Christian's duty to the State and his duty to God.

THE SERMON

> And they sent to him some of the Pharisees and some of the Herodians to entrap him in his talk. And they came and said to him, 'Teacher, we know that you are true, and care for no man; for you do not regard the position of man, but truly teach the way of God. Is it lawful to pay taxes to Caesar or not? Should we pay them or not?' But knowing their hypocrisy, he said to them, 'Why put me to the test? Bring me a coin and let me look at it.' And they brought one. And he said to them 'Whose likeness and inscription is this?' They said to him 'Caesar's.' Jesus said to them, 'Render unto Caesar the things that are Caesar's and to God the things that are God's.' And they were amazed at him [Mk. 12:13–17].

On the occasion of the Tenth Anniversary of the Nyayo Era (i.e. the rule of President Moi), when we are also meeting for the Annual Mothers' Union Rally, it is appropriate that we consider together one of the most important statements that Jesus made with regard to the relationship between the Church and State.

> 'Render unto Caesar the things that are Caesar's and to God the things that are God's.'

The Trap

Some Pharisees and Herodians were sent to Jesus to trap him in his talk. They asked him a question which they thought would put him in a very difficult situation: 'Should we pay taxes to Caesar?' Note that if Jesus answered 'Yes', his followers would have lost confidence in him and the Jewish population would have regarded him as a coward who did not even have their interests at heart, especially their freedom from Roman oppression.

One Jewish revolutionary by the name of Judas the Gaulonite had raised violent opposition against the taxation of the Jews by the Romans, telling the Jews that taxation by the Romans was no better than slavery. But the Romans had dealt with Judas efficiently and had silenced him; yet the issue he had raised remained unresolved and the people kept thinking about it. At the time of the ministry of Jesus, the zealots rallied around the slogan 'No tribute to the Romans'. The question of whether to pay taxes or not was therefore highly relevant in that area and at that time.

If on the other hand Jesus said it was not lawful to pay taxes to Caesar, his enemies would have reported him to the Roman authority and he would have been arrested and judged as a troublemaker. The Pharisees, in asking Jesus this question were sure that there was no way Jesus could get away with it. But Jesus was extremely skilful in handling the situation.

Whose Image?

'Show me a coin' Jesus asked. He was given a denarius. Note that he did not fetch out his own coin but rather he asked for theirs. 'Whose image is on the coin?' he asked them. 'Caesar's,' they answered. The image was probably that of Tiberius, the reigning emperor. And to their embarrassment, Jesus gave them this highly memorable answer: 'Render unto Caesar what is Caesar's and to God what is God's.'

The fact that the coin had the king's head and inscription on it, meant that to some extent it was the king's property. Jesus' answer therefore was something like this: 'By agreeing to use the coinage of Caesar Tiberius, you people already recognize his political power in Palestine. After all, the coinage belongs to him as it has his name on it. By giving the coin to Caesar you are giving him what belongs to him. Give the coin to Caesar as you pay the taxes. But remember that there is also another sphere of life which belongs to God and not to Caesar.'

Jesus' words have become the foundation of a vital principle which conserves at one and the same time the powers of the State and the powers of Religion. Jesus is clearly saying that credit must be given where credit is due – Caesar has every right to demand taxes. Give him what is his due – but remember that God also has an important part to play in our lives.

Render to One Another

Since this is a Mothers' Union Rally, and the Mothers' Union exists primarily to uphold the principles of Christian marriage, allow me for a moment to apply this verse to marriage. In marriage, Jesus is telling wives, 'Render to your husband what is his due.'

What does a wife render to her husband? In the wedding service, the pastor asks, '*Mary*, will you take *John* to be your husband, to live together in holy matrimony? Will you obey, serve, love, honour and keep him in sickness and in health, and will you leave all others and cling only to him?' Almost always the answer is, 'I will.' The husband is likewise told to love, comfort, honour and keep his wife. The things we pledge to render to one another are love, obedience, service, honour and comfort, at all times.

These are the things which by divine command belong to your husband and your wife. And when we exchange rings we commit ourselves to cling to one another for better, for worse, for richer for poorer, in sickness and in health, to love and to cherish until we are parted by death. In other words, we commit ourselves unconditionally. Marriage is therefore a great step of faith. You commit yourself to a person without really knowing what the future will bring. It is for better or for worse; whether there is money or no money; children or no children; incapacitating sickness or none at all. In all kinds of conditions that life may bring, you pledge to remain together.

Love, the Sole Basis of Marriage

I know a case of one sister who was about to get married to a brother in the Lord who was quite a senior bachelor. Just before the wedding day, she wrote a letter and informed the gentleman: 'By the way, before we get married there are three things I would like to satisfy myself about: I want to see your bank balance, your medical certificate, and I would further want to know whether it is in your plans to buy a car.'

Now, all these things should not really be prerequisites for marriage. In marriage, love is the binding factor. What we are meant to give one another at the time of marriage is all that we have, and that is what the ring is symbolic of. We give our bodies and all other possessions, yet even before we give all these things, we first give our love. We then start living together with a deep commitment to preserve our marriage. We accept the big challenge to go out of our way to forgive when we are wronged, to be patient, to be understanding, to continue loving even when love may appear to be going cold.

When Jesus told those Pharisees and Herodians, 'Render unto Caesar the things that are Caesar's', he was giving due recognition to the place of rulers in the lives of the people who are ruled. There are a number of issues which must be emphasized:

Organized State: God's Will

Christians must pay taxes to the state. There is no doubt that the state brings many benefits to the people. The Roman Empire brought many benefits to the ancient world, the greatest benefit being the peace it brought to many nations. People could conduct their business, provide for their families and travel anywhere without fear because of the *Pax Romana* (peace) that the Roman rule facilitated. Jesus is saying to us that no man can accept all the benefits which the state gives and then refuse the responsibility of supporting the state.

It is God's will that there should be an organized state. As Paul says, 'Let every person be subject to the governing authorities, for there is no authority except from God and those that exist have been instituted by God' (Rom. 13). God is not a God of chaos but of peace. Hence in every human institution there is need to have a leader beginning from the family. In the family the man is the head. But his headship is the headship of love. He cannot head a family as a general heads an army, issuing orders that must be obeyed without question. The woman was right who told her husband, 'If you are the head, remember I am the neck.' The head can do nothing without the neck. Men and women in families cannot live together without obeying the laws of living together.

In the same way it is within God's will that we should have the State with the president who is head. Without the State there are many things we cannot enjoy. In Embu town, no one can live on his own without the benefits of communal water, sewerage, electricity, telephone, and above all the security provided by the government to restrain evil doers. The police who have to spend many hours patrolling the streets enable us to sleep soundly without fear. Similarly the armed forces give security to the borders of this nation and make us feel that we are protected from invasion by outsiders. You cannot receive all these benefits and refuse to render to Caesar what belongs to him.

While rendering to Caesar what is his, we must also give credit where it is due. When Mzee Jomo Kenyatta died in 1978, His Excellency Daniel Arap Moi became our President. We ought to give thanks to God for the ten years President Moi has led this nation. And as we thank God for President Moi's reign, we particularly cite the following developments:

– The Nyayo wards (built through the President's fundraising efforts) in various parts of the country including Embu where we are.
– The introduction of District Focus for Development. This has given each district the power to determine its priorities through the district development committee and to take full responsibility for spending government grants.

– The Nyayo Tea zone which is meant to bring more revenue to our nation while at the same time protecting the environment around our forests.
– The introduction of the revolutionary 8–4–4 system of education in our schools.
– The introduction of Nyayo buses to ease transportation problems in our cities.
– The emphasis placed on the Nyayo philosophy of peace, love and unity.

For all these things we give credit to our beloved president and his government, and further pledge to continue giving him our dedicated support. By so doing we will be rendering to Caesar what is due to him.

In the Same Boat

We refuse to support or sympathize with any clandestine movement aimed at disturbing the peace of our nation. A story is told of two people sailing in a boat in the open sea. One of them was rowing the boat and the other was a passenger and he had a hammer and a chisel with him. He began to make a hole in the boat and when he was asked 'What are you doing?', he replied, 'Mind your own business!' But making a hole in the boat could not be described as the passenger's sole business because the imminent possibility of drowning would affect them both.

We who live in Kenya are sailing in a very big boat in open sea and if someone makes a hole in that boat, and the water enters, we shall all sink – councillors, politicians, Church leaders and everyone else. Consequently we cannot allow anyone to spoil our country.

Render to God

Jesus did not say only, 'Render to Caesar . . .', he also said, 'Render to God . . .'. In other words, Jesus is saying that Caesar must recognize his limits. The coin that Jesus was shown had Caesar's image on it and therefore it belonged to Caesar. But man is created in the image of God, and therefore we all belong to God. As Barclay puts it, 'If the State remains within its proper boundaries, and makes its proper demands, then the individual must give to it his loyalty and service; but in the last analysis, both the state and human beings belong to God and therefore, should the claims of the state and the claims of God come into conflict, then loyalty to God comes first.'

On this tenth anniversary of the Nyayo era we are grateful to the President for giving us clear assurances that our freedom of worship is fully guaranteed by the State. Secondly, to God belong such matters as justice and righteousness.

Duties of the State

The state is God's servant to ensure that justice and righteousness are exercised. If the actions of the state lack justice and righeousness, then the prophets of God must protest. If they were to keep quiet, they would be failing to render to God his due. Therefore the politicians who quote this verse so as to silence Church leaders and to prevent them from making their prophetic contribution to the prophetic life of this nation have missed the point. Rendering to Caesar what is Caesar's includes a humble and courteous reminder that all authority comes from God and should be used for God's service. In those countries where the state does not serve people and instead exploits them for the benefit of a few, the Caesars of those countries must be reminded of the justice and righteousness which God requires.

Politicans who have tried to silence Church leaders on the basis of this verse have sometimes quoted it as 'Leave' to Caesar . . .; but Jesus said 'Render . . .'. To 'leave' would imply having nothing to do with Caesar's things, to refuse even to touch his coins. But to 'render' is a positive response which involves giving every support to Caesar in areas where he has legitimate authority. Neither can we leave Caesar alone to handle matters that concern all of us. As it has been said, politics is so important in human life that it cannot be left to professional politicians alone.

In conclusion we must do everything possible to protect family life and to bring up our children in the right way. But we also have a duty to render to God our absolute obedience and worship.

God Bless our Nation.

God Bless our families!

11

St Stephen

A topical sermon preached at the opening of St Stephen's Evangelistic Training Centre, Marsabit on 11 June 1989.

THE SERMON

We have gathered here today so that we may honour one of the greatest men in Christian history – Stephen, who is first mentioned in Acts 6:5.

When the apostles found that they were spending too much time in serving tables instead of preaching the gospel, they decided to choose seven deacons, and Stephen's name was on the top of the list. He is described as a man full of faith and the Holy Spirit. It is important to note that the men who were appointed deacons were carefully selected and although they were men of humble service, i.e. to serve tables, they were supposed to be men of wisdom, faith, and full of the Holy Spirit. This selection criteria is very important for the Church even today and should be applied even in our local Church Annual General Meetings when electing the Church Committee members.

Many of the leadership wrangles we experience today in our Churches are a result of electing people who lack wisdom and whose faith and spirituality are questionable. Their main desire is to be in positions of leadership and not really to serve God's people.

We have many examples in this regard but the most outstanding I can think of so far is what took place at Kamugunda Church in Kirinyaga district. Thumaita Parish had just been created from Ngariama Parish and it was only logical that the young congregration at nearby Kamugunda should join Thumaita Church to form the new Thumaita Parish. But one of the leaders at Kamugunda rejected the move simply because the Thumaita people had refused to elect him as the chairman of the local primary school committee. When it became clear that he could not win the case, and knowing well that he would not get a leadership post in the new parish, he opted out of the Church of the Province of Kenya and joined the Presbyterian Church to which he gave a portion of his land on which to build a Church, of course with very high hopes that he would be given a significant post in the Church.

People of faith, and who are full of wisdom and the Holy Spirit are guided not so much by what they can gain but what they can offer. Some people may have complained about the positioning of different development projects in the diocese. Some have expressed concern as to which Archdeaconry the St Paul's Cathedral should be in. But the Cathedral is for the whole Diocese and every archdeaconry has a claim to the Cathedral for it was built by Christians from every corner of the Diocese. People of faith and wisdom will seek peace and not disunity in the Church of Christ.

Stephen confronts Jews

This man who was elected to serve tables, had some other qualities: he was richly blessed by God; he was full of power; he had the gift of healing and he did miracles and wonders among the people. I guess that Stephen found the ministry of serving tables rather boring and before very long he was on the streets preaching the Gospel. He was certainly talented in preaching and debating. Eventually, he began to meet opposition from some men who were members of the Synagogue of freed men, that is, Jews who had been taken prisoners in Rome by Pompey and later freed. They returned to Jerusalem and built their own synagogue because they were Greek speaking.

Stephen's arguments were so powerful that they could not defeat him. We read in Acts 6:10 that the Spirit gave Stephen such wisdom that when he spoke they could not refute him.

History has shown us that whenever a talented leader emerges, the more influential he becomes, the more opposition he encounters. Those of us who are leaders, whether in politics or the Church, should always remember that the harder we work to serve the people, the more certain sections of people will look for errors to point out.

When Moses delivered the Jews from oppression in Egypt, one would naturally expect them to be thankful throughout. Yet we see that in their journey through the desert, far away from Egypt, the Israelites complained bitterly against Moses for taking them out of Egypt and 'bringing us to suffer in the desert'. Even after being fed with manna from heaven, they still opposed him.

Daniel was such an able and efficient administrator that the king even wanted to appoint him as prime minister. But the government ministers did not like this because Daniel was a Jew. So the ministers plotted to have a new law enacted which they were sure Daniel could not obey, and so he would subsequently be overthrown. They persuaded the king to make a stupid law that for thirty days no one would be permitted to request anything from any god or from any man except from the king (Dan. 6:6–9).

They knew very well that Daniel could not obey such a law. Daniel continued to pray to the God of heaven with his window wide open. The enemies reported him to the king, and very reluctantly the king ordered Daniel to be put in the den of lions but his God never abandoned him and he was not even touched by the lions. The following day the king went early to the den and found Daniel still alive and moving around. The king ordered Daniel to be taken out of the den and that all those who had opposed him be put into the den; they were devoured as soon as they landed in the den.

This story of Daniel shows clearly how easily the king's advisors can destabilize the state by misleading the leader. Why make a law for the king to be worshipped for only thirty days? Why not forever? And for heaven's sake, why make a law that is aimed at only one person – Daniel the prime minister, knowing so well that Daniel would never bow to any other god except God? This reminds us of an incident in 1976 when some big people in the government attempted to change the constitution so that the then vice-president, Daniel Arap Moi, could not succeed the former president Kenyatta when the latter died. But the President in his wisdom rejected the advice of those men because they were driven by sheer selfishness and hunger for power and wanted the shortest means possible to achieve the desired results.

Stephen is accused (Acts:11)

When the members of the Synagogue of freed men and other Jews from Cilicia and Asia found Stephen such an able debater, and that he could not be beaten in arguments, they bribed some people with money to make serious allegations against him. 'We heard him speak against Moses and against God! . . . This man is always talking against our sacred temple and the Law of Moses. . . . We heard him say that Jesus of Nazareth will tear down the temple – change all customs which have come down to us from Moses' (Acts 6:11, 13, 14).

Stephen was taken before the Sanhedrin, the supreme council and highest court of justice. In New Testament times it consisted of 71 members, drawn from the priestly aristocracy and from the ranks of the Scribes and the Pharisees. The supreme office belonged to the High Priest. Accusations against Stephen were highly exaggerated and his speeches largely misquoted. Misquotation of sermons is not a new phenomenon.

After all the accusations, Stephen was given a chance to defend himself. The whole of Acts 7 is Stephen's famous defence which took the form of an account of the salvific history of the Jewish people right from the time of Abraham to the time of Jesus in whom and through whom the final work of salvation was fulfilled.

In this defence Stephen insists that men worshipped God long before there was a temple, and that God does not dwell in temples built by men. He also argued that when the Jews crucified Jesus they were only following what they had always done before by persecuting the prophets and abandoning the leaders appointed by God. These were hard truths for men who believed themselves to be chosen people and it is no wonder that they were infuriated.

Undiplomatic Stephen

Though Stephen was a man of faith and wisdom he seems to have lacked one thing: diplomacy. In our preaching we must be careful that we do not communicate the truth undiplomatically when the situation demands otherwise. Perhaps the tension that sometimes occurs between Church leaders and politicians is a result of lack of diplomacy in our pulpit communication.

Paul told Timothy to preach in season and out of season, and with all patience. Stephen's lack of diplomacy came to a climax when he called the Jewish elders sitting in the high court, 'uncircumcised'. The worst thing you can do to a Jew is to call him uncircumcised. The infuriated Jews took Stephen away into a valley where they inflicted mob (in)justice on him by throwing stones on him until he died. Stephen was obviously not accorded a proper trial.

The Blood of Martyrs is Seed

The secret behind Stephen's courage was that beyond all that men could do to him, he saw awaiting him the welcome of his Lord. He saw the martyr's death as a gateway to heaven. And just as his Master Jesus Christ had prayed for his persecutors, Stephen too prayed: 'Lord, do not remember this sin against them.' The whole turmoil finished and with a strange peace he fell asleep.

Saul (later Paul) at that time was at the forefront of the killing of believers, and indeed he seems to have largely masterminded Stephen's death. But soon after Stephen's death, and on one of his missions to fight against the faith, the Lord met him, overturned his deadly plans and made him an apostle. The blood of martyrs is truly seed. Stephen was the first martyr in the history of the Church and we might be right to say that Saul, the famous tyrant, was the first significant seed that came sprouting from Stephen's blood, and with him, many Gentiles.

Dedication in Remembrance

In remembrance of St Stephen, we have gathered here to dedicate this centre to God for the training of evangelists. It has been built first and foremost in memory of the first martyr in Christian history. The centre commemorates also the life and ministry of the late Canon Stephen Houghton who served the people of Marsabit as a BCMS missionary from 1960 until he was called home to be with the Lord on 17th April 1983. It is our prayer that those who come here to be trained as evangelists will follow in the footsteps of St Stephen, a man of faith and wisdom and full of the Holy Spirit; a man richly blessed by God and full of power; a man who could perform great miracles and wonders among the people; an able preacher and debater, and above all a very courageous man.

An evangelist who is timid is a contradiction in terms. As St Paul told Timothy, 'the spirit that God has given us does not make us timid; instead his spirit fills us with power and love and self control' [2 Tim.1:7]. We hope that out of this centre will emerge evangelists who are so courageous that they will proclaim the whole truth and preach the gospel regardless of possible consequences, even death; for beyond death, we see Jesus!

12

God of Order, not of Confusion

1 Corinthians 14:33

A sermon preached on 2nd April 1989 during a Confirmation Service at St Mary's Church, Mugumo, Kirinyaga.

THE SETTING

Around this time, a crisis had occurred in relations between the Diocese of Mount Kenya East, and local political and administrative authorities in Kirinyaga District. The crisis had both a local and a national dimension. The national dimension was connected with the Bishop's outspokenness on prevailing controversies such as the just-ended Kiharu by-election, and the political woes surrounding the then Vice-President, Dr Josphat Karanja. However, the local dimension was of more fundamental importance in this crisis.

The previous year had seen remarkable shifts in the political alliances in Kirinyaga. The new MP for Ndia Constituency, who was also the Minister for National Guidance and Political Affairs, Mr James Njiru, had supported Mr Geoffrey Kariithi in the General Election of February 1988. Mr Kariithi was consequently elected as the MP for Gichugu Constituency. However, by the time of the Kanu party elections in September, Mr Njiru had switched his support to Kariithi's long-term rival, Mr Nahashon Njuno. As a result Mr Njuno won the Kanu sub-branch chairmanship in Gichugu.

The common factor in both elections was the blatant rigging of votes and the intimidation of voters. Although the Bishop had pledged to work in co-operation with any de facto *leaders, he was considerably alarmed by the extreme abuse of justice that characterized the elections, in which the local administration officials were heavily implicated.*

Almost all public figures in Kirinyaga had been cowed into silence regarding these evils, because their jobs were at the mercy of the politicians and administrators.

Earlier in the year the Kirinyaga District Commissioner, Mr Joseph Mengich, had refused the Bishop a permit to conduct a fundraising exercise for Githure, a Diocesan sponsored Secondary School. A contingent of policemen were sent to the school to ensure that no fundraising took place. During the same week, a public meeting to welcome the newly appointed Provincial Commissioner Mr Victor Musoga became chaotic as Chiefs were attacked and a Member of Parliament shouted down by Kanu youth wingers.

The last time the Bishop had visited Mugumo Parish was in April 1988 when he got a very cold reception from the Christians. This was mainly because of an article in the magazine, Beyond *where the Bishop was quoted as having said that elections in Gichugu had been rigged in favour of Mr Kariithi, who apparently comes from St. Mary's Church, Mugumo.*

For many years Mr Geoffrey Kariithi had been the Chairman of the Christian Community Services of the Diocese of Mt Kenya East. However, the Bishop had made it clear that nothing was going to stop him from exposing election malpractices, even if close friends were involved. The Christians of Mugumo received the Bishop coldly, assuming that he was simply being partisan, that he would possibly have been happier if Kariithi's opponent, Mr Nahashon Njuno had won. They were yet to realize that the Bishop was upholding a principle, that no election should be rigged against anyone.

One evening in August 1988, Nahashon Njuno visited the Bishop at his Difathas home and informed him that he was sure to recapture the Gichugu sub-branch chairmanship because the Hon. James Njiru had already taken him to State House and he had been given a vehicle and money for campaigning. When the Bishop remarked that G. K. Kariithi had apparently become more popular than he was, Mr Njuno stood his ground and said he had assurance from both Mr Njiru and the Civil administration that the elections would be rigged in his (Njuno's) favour and there was no chance of Kariithi winning. The bishop informed him that if that was the case he would publicly expose the scandal and challenge his election.

In September 1988, Kanu grassroot and Branch elections were held, and Mr Kariithi was removed from the chairmanship of Gichugu sub-branch through vote rigging. The Bishop once again spoke firmly and openly against the rigged elections in which Mr Nahashon Njuno had emerged the winner. And so when the Bishop visited St. Mary's Mugumo on 2nd April 1989, he received a V.I.P treatment for having upheld the principle that elections should not be rigged.

THE SERMON

1. Introduction

The Church in Corinth was very charismatic and members put much emphasis on the gifts of the Holy Spirit. However, these gifts were not being used in the right way. And so, in 1Corinthians, Paul dedicates three chapters, 12, 13 and 14, to teaching on the right use of the gifts of the Holy Spirit. He identified nine gifts of the Holy Spirit which the Christians in Corinth were exercising: the utterance of wisdom, the utterance of knowledge, faith, healing, working miracles, prophecy, ability to distinguish between spirits, speaking in tongues, and interpretation of tongues [1 Cor.12:8–11].

Paul did not see anything wrong in Christians having these gifts; but he was concerned that they were being manipulated. Some people thought that because they had certain gifts they were more spiritual than other people who did not have them. As a result they became proud, and the consequence was disunity in the Church.

2. Spiritual Gifts

Paul said whatever gift one has is to be used for the common good of the whole Church. Just as in a human body there are different parts with different functions, so must all the gifts of the Holy Spirit be used for the good of the Church. Likewise, God has appointed leaders with different offices in the Church, who must all work together for the common good of the Body of Christ.

The problem in the Corinthian Church was that people who had the gift of speaking in tongues felt that they were spiritually more important than people with other gifts. But Paul told them that the one who prophesies is indeed more important than the one who speaks in tongues because the purpose of speaking in tongues is self-edification, but a prophet ministers to the whole Church. The prophet proclaims the gospel in such a way that the hearers are built up, encouraged and consoled [1 Cor. 14:3].

Paul said that though he himself spoke in tongues more than anyone else, when he came to Church he would rather speak five words which people could understand than many words which nobody could understand. The biggest problem however was that those who spoke in tongues did so simultaneously, thus making the Church a very noisy place. Paul warned them: 'If, then, the whole Church meets together and everyone starts speaking in strange tongues – and if some ordinary people or unbelievers come in, won't they say that you are all crazy?' [1 Cor. 14:23].

He gave instructions on how the gifts were to be used. Firstly, he said, if the Corinthians wanted to speak in tongues, then it should only be a few people, one at a time, and there must be an interpreter, otherwise they should keep quiet. Secondly, Paul told them that even those with gifts of prophecy should prophesy one by one, so that all might learn. He concluded: 'For God is not a God of confusion, but of peace' [14:33]. A very important characteristic of God is revealed here; that he is a God of peace and order.

3. Leadership in Society

In order that there might be order throughout human society, God has appointed leaders in every area of life. In the family, for example, the man is the head of the household. If both the husband and the wife were to assume headship, then confusion would reign in that home. God has appointed the husband to be the head, and he expects him to use that headship responsibly. Similarly, we acknowledge proper authorities in every institution. Every hospital has its superintendent, every school its head, every college a principal, every class a prefect, every army unit a commanding officer, and so on. The Church too has its structures of authority. The same is true of national administration as a whole. Where there is no leader, the result is anarchy.

a. Leadership With Respect

To preserve the order and peace which God desires, leaders must be both respected and obeyed. In 1 Thessalonians, Paul instructs his readers: 'We beg you, our brothers, to pay proper respect to those who work among you, who guide and instruct you in the Christian life. Treat them with the greatest respect because of the work they do. Be at peace among yourselves' [5:12–13]. Once a person has been appointed to lead others, he deserves to be respected. And in the area of national leadership, the greatest respect and honour must be accorded to our President.

b. Quality Leadership

When Jethro visited his son-in-law, Moses, in the desert, he found that Moses was judging Israel all alone. And so he advised him to select qualified leaders to help him: capable men who were God-fearing, trustworthy and incorruptible [Ex. 18:21–22]. The process of selection of leaders is very important. For leaders to command respect, they must be chosen in accordance with the constitutional stipulations of the particular institution. The leaders must also have the interests of the people at heart. For example, when our President realized that coffee farmers had not been paid anything for six months, he directed that Ksh1.2 billion be paid out to the farmers at once. This came as a great relief to those families whose children had been suspended from school because they were unable to pay school fees. Leaders should have a genuine concern for the poor, the oppressed and the hungry. In fact, I must state here that leaders are not to be obeyed unconditionally. During ordination, the ordinand vows to obey his bishop 'in all things lawful'. Leaders should not expect us to obey them when they give unlawful commands.

4. Confusion

God appoints leaders in society to avoid the danger of confusion. However, just as St Paul found the Church in Corinth in a state of confusion, we too are confused in a number of areas: a) When a civil servant is at liberty to attack government ministers publicly, without being reprimanded, we get confused. Civil servants are expected to respect and honour those who are above them. b) When a public meeting to welcome a new Provincial Commissioner becomes a forum for attacking Chiefs, and shouting down a duly elected Member of Parliament, we get confused. What good does it serve, to show the new PC how good we are at attacking duly elected leaders, instead of concentrating on the important agenda? c) When a government minister alleges that a Church leader is interfering with Kanu, yet does not tell us who that Church leader is, we are confused. Of course we know very well who, and why he is being attacked. If by 'interfering' he is referring to our challenge over the rigged Kanu (party) elections in Kirinyaga, then Kanu can expect such 'interference' to continue. However, Kanu itself is to blame for interfering with people's constitutional right to elect leaders of their choice. d) When an assistant chief grabbed the microphone from Bishop Alexander Muge as he was preaching to worshippers at St Emanuel Church Mutira, we were astounded; and worse still, the Provincial Commissioner went on to deny that anything like that had happened, thus leaving us confused and in no doubt that there is a leadership crisis in this country. Hundreds of people were eye-witnesses of what happened; and thousands, probably millions, saw the photographs of the incident in the newspapers. Ours is not a God of confusion, but of order and peace. e) When a District Commissioner deliberately refuses us a licence to conduct a *harambee* and goes on to impose all sorts of pre-conditions that we do not accept and when he finally asks us to look for a different Guest of Honour instead of the Diocesan Bishop, we get confused. Further, this D.C. even dared to tell the whole nation that we were 'demanding preferential treatment and were impatient'. There are too many contradictory statements coming from a leader who expects to be respected and obeyed! f) When one individual thinks he has the indisputable mandate to determine people's political destiny, thus denying us the opportunity to exercise the very rights for which Kenyans fought and won at independence, we get very confused. We are being tossed about by the political whims of one person; on one occasion he influences an election in favour of 'M'; the next time he does the same in favour of 'N'. This is confusion; and our God is not a God of confusion.

5. Peace

We have the duty to preserve peace in the district and in the nation; and the way of peace, (as I have said elsewhere) is not the passive acceptance of things. The way of peace is to confront situations and seek to correct things where they have gone wrong; it is to reconcile warring forces and hence avert situations that would otherwise be counter productive. In all this, a lot of patience is necessary, even when it is tested to its limits. We have a crucial duty to pray for our leaders, that they might allow God to clean up the mess they have made of politics and put their house in order. He is a God of order, not of confusion. We too must repent and ask God to forgive us for whatever we may have done to allow confusion to creep into certain aspects of our political governance. Let us work for order in our individual lives, and in society as a whole. For God is not the author of confusion but of order and peace, Amen.

13

Blessed Are the Peacemakers

Matthew 5:9

A sermon preached at St. Thomas' Church, Kerugoya, on Sunday, 9th April 1989, during a special service of thanksgiving and prayers.

THE SETTING

At this time the country was witnessing one of the most blatant election malpractices, when in the full glare of national publicity, a by-election held in Kiharu, Muranga was rigged in favour of Kanu's choice, Mr Mweru. The incumbent area MP, Mr Kenneth Matiba had dramatically resigned his cabinet post and was subsequently expelled from Kanu. On the television one could see a visibly shaken Dr Gikonyo Kiano (the other contestant) who found the dishonesty too blatant to accept. His rival, Mr Mweru, had been announced the winner although it was evident that far fewer people had queued to support him than the number who supported Mr Kiano. Subsequently, several Church leaders, including the Bishop, loudly denounced this malpractice.

It may have been this controversy, as well as other murky issues of Kirinyaga District politics, that prompted the Gichugu Kanu sub-branch Chairman, Mr Nahashon Njuno, to announce that he intended to summon the Bishop before the Kanu Branch to answer unspecified charges. The Bishop accepted the summons which he saw as an opportunity to talk face to face with Gichugu leaders about the right way to conduct political debate. This reaction disappointed the party, so they decided to apply a different method of intimidation. As a result, some youth wingers were hired to come and heckle the Bishop if he ever mentioned Kanu in his sermon. Indeed two of the scoundrels dared to do so but were dragged out of the Church, while the congregation of about 6,000 people stood solidly with the Bishop.

THE SERMON

Jesus said to his disciples in his parting message: 'Peace I leave with you, my peace I give you, not as the world gives do I give you. Let not your hearts be troubled, neither let them be afraid' [Jn. 14:27].[1] At the point of departure the greatest thing that Jesus could leave his beloved friends (who had intimately walked with him for the last three years) was Peace [*Shalom* in Hebrew, or *Eirene* in Greek].

The word, peace, is generally used to describe the end of war or trouble. If a country has been undergoing a period of civil war and then all those who have been fighting lay down their arms, we would say that peace has returned to that country, despite the fact that the land is devastated, cities are in ruins, and men and women and children are starving. But the Hebrew word for peace, *shalom*, has a far wider meaning than that. It describes perfect welfare, serenity, prosperity and happiness. To greet a person with *shalom* is to wish him everything which makes for his contentment and his good. *Shalom* also describes right personal relationships – it describes uninterrupted goodwill between two people. Therefore in Hebrew thought peace does not describe only the absence of war and strife; peace describes happiness, and well-being in life, and perfection of human relationships. When the psalmist asks that peace should be within the walls of Jerusalem:

> Pray for the peace of Jerusalem: they shall prosper that love thee. Peace be within thy walls and prosperity within thy palaces. For my brethren and companions' sakes, I will now say, 'Peace be within thee' [Ps. 122:6–8]

his desire is that every good blessing should descend upon the city and its citizens. The Greek word for peace, *Eirene* occurs 88 times in the New Testament and it is found in each of the 27 books of the New Testament. One of the great characteristics of the New Testament letters is that they begin and end with a prayer for peace for those who read the letters. Hence Paul begins his letter to the Philippians: 'May God our Father and the Lord Jesus Christ give you grace and peace.'

Practical *Shalom*

'Blessed are the peacemakers for they shall be called sons of God' [Mt. 5:9]. Some of my friends have advised me that if the Gichugu Kanu branch summons me . . . (*as soon as the bishop mentioned Kanu, a youth winger later to be identified as Mr Gerald Mwai Kibaki began to push his way forward and heckled him. He was restrained by ushers from making further advances. Meanwhile the congregation spontaneously sprung up with the hymn 'Tukutendereza Yesu' as the intruder was ushered out of the Church. Then as the bishop resumed his sermon from where he had stopped, a second heckler identified as Njeru Ndiruchi, alias General Waguthira stood up and began to interrupt. Once again the mammoth congregation of about 6000 people burst into songs of praise and victory against the devil, while the ushers restrained the heckler whom they kept under close watch while the service continued*).

---

1. For a fuller treatment of the biblical concepts of peace, peace-makers and peace-lovers see other chapters in this book.

. . .And so (went on the Bishop), before I was interrupted I was saying that some of my dear friends have advised me that if the Gichugu Kanu sub branch summons me I should not attend so as to avoid the discomfort of being put in dock. But the way of peace is not in evading Kanu. When the day comes, I shall wear my red cassock, and the clergy in their black robes shall escort me. We shall appear before Kanu and I hope we shall be given a chance to share our concerns in regard to recent developments in the party. Together we can face the issues and seek ways and means of bringing about reconciliation.

Shalom means welfare and well-being at their best and at their highest. Therefore this beatitude means that all those who do anything to increase the well-being and the welfare of the world are blessed. Social transformation is the work of God. Those who do anything to make life in the world fuller and happier and easier for others are truly serving God. Those who zealously toil to conquer the problem of unemployment are peacemakers. The scientists who are working round the clock to find a cure for AIDS and other deadly diseases are peacemakers because healing and conquering pain brings about *shalom*. Those who toil so that the hungry may be fed and the poor and the old cared for are peacemakers. When the president initiates the fund-raising drive for the disabled in the country and helps to raise over 70 million shillings, he is a peacemaker. When he hears the cries of coffee farmers and directs that they be paid their long outstanding dues, isn't he a peacemaker? When tea farmers cry out that they are losing many kilos of picked tea-leaves because of delays in delivery to the factories, and someone hears those cries and responds positively, isn't that the way of peace? Any man or woman with a passion for the welfare of those around him, is rendering service to God and in so doing he is blessed. Such are the people Jesus was talking about when he said:

> Come you that are blessed by my Father, come and possess the kingdom which has been prepared for you ever since the creation of the world. For I was hungry and you fed me, I was thirsty and you gave me a drink, I was a stranger and you received me in your homes, I was naked and you clothed me, I was sick and you took care of me, I was in prison and you visited me. . . . I tell you whenever you did this for one of the least important of these brothers and sisters of mine, you did it for me [Mt. 25:34–36, 40]

Shalom and Relationships

We get even nearer to the meaning of this beatitude when we see *shalom* as right relationships. The Jewish rabbis thought that those who honour father and mother, those who do good, and those who make peace between people reap good fruits alike in this life and in the life to come. A person lives in three dimensions of relationships - relationship with himself, with his fellow men and with God. A Bible commentator has observed that man is in himself a walking civil war. There is always within him a battle between the desires of the flesh and the desires of the spirit. And for a man of God this fact is a painful one, as Paul observed: 'I do not understand what I do. For what I want to do, I do not do, but what I hate, I do' [Rom. 7:15]. We know that we are at one time capable of an almost saintly goodness while at another time we are capable of an almost devilish evil. At one time we are capable of sacrificial kindness and at another time we are extremely unkind to other people. There is continuous tension within us. Hence a person is a walking civil war, never knowing which side will win victory. Paul says, 'I live, yet not I, but Christ lives in me' [Gal. 2:20]. Once we allow Christ to come and live in us, then Christ, the author of peace, brings peace to us. Blessed indeed is the man who is at peace with himself, the man in whom contradictions are obliterated, the man whose inner battle has been stilled in the control of Christ. One of the most notable sayings of St Augustine of Hippo was 'Thou hast made us for thyself, and our hearts are restless until they find their rest (peace) in thee'.

We live in a divided world, with its iron curtains, lines of demarcation, its division between races, nations and tribes, and even clans. Here in this diocese I have seen sharp divisions between Mururi and Ndamata clans of Mbeere. There was also a time when the Gichugu people were divided 'mathematically' between 21 and 42. And in Mwea, there is a tendency for people to divide themselves according to the nature of the soil - black soil and red soil. Note that rice can only be grown in black cotton soil while maize and other crops are grown in red soil. So the division is between rice growers and other farmers. Now, politically there has also been a tendency to divide people between those who are said to be true Nyayo followers and those who are not. But if Nyayo philosophy stands for peace, love and unity, I would like to state that regardless of where they classify you, you remain a true Nyayo follower, if you are working for peace in the spirit of love by struggling against all kinds of injustice.

The greatest need of the people of Kirinyaga, and indeed the people of Kenya, is the cultivation of right relationships with one another. We must work to remove all that which divides us if we want to lay a deserved claim to *shalom*. Where there is division we need to work for reconciliation. True reconciliation does not come by sweeping problems under the carpet or by a mere shaking of hands in public places. We must find the root cause of our divisions and deal with it. The Christian must labour to produce right relationships between people. In any society there are two types of people – those who have a disruptive influence and those who have a reconciling influence. Christian reconciliation means reconciling people to God and reconciling people to each other. A reconciler must not take sides except when it is the side of the truth.

Relationship With God

Both the Old and the New Testaments emphasize the fact that God is the author of peace. In the Book of Numbers, Moses is instructed by the Lord to give Aaron and his sons the words they will use in blessing the people:

> The Lord bless you and keep you.
> The Lord make his face to shine upon you
> The Lord lift up his countenance upon you and give you peace [Nu. 6:24–26].

Jesus tells his disciples, 'Peace I leave with you.' But God does not give his peace unconditionally. There are two conditions. The first is to obey God's commandments.

> O that you had hearkened to my commandments.
> Then your peace would have been like a river, and your righteousness like the waves of the sea [Isa. 48:18].

Thus Isaiah says:

> Then justice will dwell in the wilderness
> and righteousness abide in the fruitful field.
> And the effect of righteousness will be peace, and the result of righteousness, quietness and trust for ever [Isa. 32:16–17].

Justice and righteousness as conditions for peace are central themes in the preaching of the prophets. Micah, Jeremiah and Ezekiel engaged in conflict with false prophets on the question of peace. The false prophets promised peace when the conditions of peace were not fulfilled. But the prophets were insistent that there could be no peace unless Israel turned away from evil. While false prophets continued to say, 'Peace, peace', Jeremiah emphasized that there cannot be peace while injustices continue unabated. 'Everyone was greedy for unjust gain; they were stubbornly rebellious; all of them acted corruptly' [Jer. 6:13, 28].

No Intimidation

Often we see leaders silencing people through intimidation; yet this does not work for true peace. You may suppress the tongue but not the mind; and in due course the mind will insist on expressing itself. And certainly that will not work for peace.

Sons of God

Those that are prepared to confront crises and work for peace despite the risk involved are peacemakers. And they are blessed because they are engaged in the very task that God himself is involved in. And for that reason they shall be called sons of God! I call upon all Christians to participate actively in the task of peace-making. In conclusion, do not worry about anything, but in all your prayers ask God for what you need, always asking him with a thankful heart. And God's peace which is far beyond human understanding, will keep your hearts and minds safe in union with Christ Jesus. *SHALOM*.

14

Duties of the State and Obligations of Citizens

1 Peter 2: 13–17

Sermon Preached on 30th April 1989 at St. Thomas' Cathedral, Kerugoya.

THE SETTING

After the occasion of April 9th, on which the Bishop was heckled, the atmosphere in Kirinyaga District grew increasingly tense. Although the two hecklers were well-known, the police seemed powerless to arrest them. This apparent 'immunity' made 'General Waguthira' bold enough to accost the Bishop and his clergy companions in a Kerugoya street in broad daylight the following Saturday. Several administration officials stood by and took no action.

Eventually the police came and took Waguthira away; but later the same night a number of Chiefs led by D.O. Ndia Division came to the police station and demanded his release. It was not surprising that the local Kanu officials failed to condemn these misdeeds. Apparently they were more concerned to condemn what they saw as the Bishop's anti-party stance. Hence they made several allegations against him which were extremely insulting and disturbing and made no effort to substantiate them.

During the following week a group of political activists in Kirinyaga told the press that there was a plot to attack and burn the Bishop's car and property. The informers were arrested and charged with making a false report, and were subsequently detained for a month at King'ong'o prison in Nyeri. Soon after, on the night of 22nd–23rd April, the Bishop's house was attacked by a large gang of thugs armed with pangas and iron bars. They cut the telephone wires, smashed the windows and tore down the security grills. The Bishop, his wife Grace, the Rev. Andrew Adano and the Bishop's eldest son, Sammy, all escaped onto the roof of the house. The two younger sons and a friend who was staying with them bravely remained in the lower part of the house with the thugs, and, in effect, prevented them from following the others onto the roof.

As the thugs prowled around, shouting, 'We have come to finish the Bishop', the Bishop, from the rooftop, called out to the neighbours for help. Sammy managed to jump down to the ground and escaped to telephone the police. Neighbours arrived, armed with whatever weapons they could lay their hands on. This foiled the deadly mission of the thugs and they fled.

Eight days later, the Diocese held a service of prayers and thanksgiving to God for the Bishop's deliverance. The service was attended by a record congregation of 15,000 people and the Bishop preached three short sermons. In the third sermon the Bishop addressed the fundamental problem of the state's obligations to its citizens and vice versa. The Bishop strongly believed that the attack on his house could never have taken place had the authorities responded promptly to the earlier troubles. If the authorities cannot protect a public figure such as a bishop, this reduces the confidence of every other citizen in the State's protection against evil.

THE SERMON

> Be subject for the Lord's sake to every human institution, whether it be to the Emperor as supreme, or to the governors as sent by him to punish those who do wrong and to praise those who do right. For it is God's will that by doing right you should put to silence the ignorance of foolish men. Live as free men, yet without using your freedom as a pretext for evil; but live as servants of God. Honour all men. Love the brotherhood, fear God, honour the Emperor [1 Pet. 2:13–17].

In this passage, St Peter gives us some guidelines on how a Christian ought to relate to the social institutions of an ordered society. These may include a family, a school, a farmers' society, a company, or the state itself. The actual human arrangements of these may vary considerably from place to place and from age to age. What Christians ought to recognize is that in their general character such institutions are in harmony with God's will for the ordering of human life. Christians should therefore fulfil their duties to these human institutions. This is mainly because the existence of such institutions is based on divine initiative. Paul puts it even more directly in Romans 13:1, when he says: 'Let every person be subject to the governing authorities; for there is no authority except from God, and those that exist have been instituted by God'. Because God is not the God of chaos but of order and peace, it is he who gives power to the governing authorities. In any human institution, there is a recognized leader. In a family, God has appointed the husband to be the head. In a village we have an assistant chief; in a location, a chief; in a Division, a DO; in a District, a DC; in a province, a PC; and in a state, a President. If there were no such leaders, there would be catastrophic anarchy. But our God is not a God of anarchy; he is not a God of confusion. And so the governing authorities are there with the authority of God; and consequently we have a duty to be subject to them. It is for this reason that we can confidently say it is by God's will that His Excellency Daniel Arap Moi, is our President at this particular time in the history of our country.

Subject Yourselves for the Lord's Sake

To be subject to the governing authorities signifies a voluntary subordination of oneself to others, putting the interests and welfare of others above one's own, preferring to give rather than to receive, to serve rather than to be served. It means giving ourselves to and for others. We do this, not for our own sake, but for the Lord's sake. We do not subject ourselves to others for any selfish motives: it is for the Lord's sake.The Christian, though his citizenship is in heaven, is also a citizen of a particular earthly state. Therefore a Christian, as a citizen of an earthly state, must recognize the lawful claims of the State and his obligation to his neighbour. Peter insists that the Christian must be subject to the King (or Roman Emperor) as the supreme power, and to the governors sent by him.

In our own situation the Christian is subject not only to the President of this country, but also those to whom he has given authority to rule over us because their authority too comes from God. Remember that when Peter wrote his epistle, Nero was the Emperor and he was not at all a good emperor. So the citizen's obligation does not depend on the personal goodness of the ruler, but on the office he holds.

However, the Church has a duty to keep reminding those in authority that their authority comes from God. According to Peter, the main purpose of the State, as intended by God, is the punishment of evil-doers, and the praise of them that do well. Elsewhere Paul makes a similar point when he says: 'For rulers are not a terror to good conduct, but to bad. Would you have no fear of him who is in authority? Then do what is good, then you will receive his approval, for he is God's servant for your good. But if you do wrong, be afraid of him: for he does not bear the sword in vain. He is the servant of God to execute his wrath on the wrongdoers' [Rom. 13:3–4].

One of the main purposes of an organized State is to restrain the disruptive and chaotic tendencies of man's self-assertion against his neighbour. The State has a duty to discourage evil-doing by punishing the evil-doers; it has a duty to encourage good conduct by praising those who do good. For this reason we have (in a well organized State), the law-making arm, or Parliament; we have the executive arm of the government, which ensures that the decisions of the law makers are implemented; we have the judiciary, which has the duty of punishing evil doers and ensuring that justice is done.

All that notwithstanding, we know that man's nature is fallen. Consequently, even in the most civilized society there are evil doers such as Paul describes in the letter to the Romans: 'They are filled with all manner of wickedness, evil, covetousness, strife, deceit, malignity, they are gossips, slanderers, haters of God, insolent, haughty, boastful, inventors of evil, disobedient to parents, foolish, faithless, heartless, ruthless. Though they know God's decree that those who do such things deserve to die, they not only do them but approve those who practise them' [Rom. 1:28–30]. In a world filled with such people, law-abiding citizens cannot live at peace unless they are protected. For this reason we have the police. The presence of the police anywhere helps to restrain the evil-doers from committing crimes. As long as good citizens are assured that evil-doers will be restrained by the strong arm of those who implement the law, then they can enjoy peace and tranquillity. And in the eyes of God, the State will be fulfilling its great purpose, or as Peter puts it, 'the vengeance of evil-doers and the praise of them that do good'. The evil-doers include not only common thieves, robbers and murderers, but also their masters who plan the evil and then recruit the criminals to carry out their projects. The evil-doers include those who work day and night to plan schemes for overthrowing a legitimately elected government.

As I have said repeatedly before, Christian men and women cannot accept any subversive activities by anyone, whether based in the country or outside the country. If we have any grievances, we would rather express them openly and without fear, than go underground. As for those issuing press statements, accusing me of such activities, let them know that my conscience is absolutely clear, and I am prepared for any fair investigation, and I am confident that in the final analysis the truth will be triumphant. But we must remember that evil-doers could also include those who ignore the established and agreed constitutional procedures of a democratic country and seek to gain power by devious ways and without the authority of the people. The conduct of evil-doers was described by the prophet Micah when he said:

> 'Woe to those who devise wickedness and work evil upon their beds; when the morning dawns they perform it, because it is in the power of their hands. They covet fields and seize them, and houses and take them away. They oppress a man and his house, a man and his inheritance' [Mic. 2:1–2].

But as long as evil-doers are apprehended and punished, then the State will be fulfilling what Peter considers to be its main task.

What worried the prophet Habakkuk most was that the State in his time was not punishing evil-doers.

> 'O Lord, how long shall I cry for help and thou will not hear, or cry to thee "Violence" and thou wilt not save? Why dost thou make me see wrongs and look upon trouble? Destruction and violence are before me, strife and contention arise, so the law is slacked and justice never goes forth; the wicked surround the righteous, so justice goes forth perverted' [Hab. 1:2–4].

These words echo the dark days of 1969 when the people of Central Kenya were forced to take an oath which was popularly euphemised as *Chai* (tea) and whose aim was mainly to promote tribal feelings much against our conscience. In the midst of this chaos the police were helpless, because the *Chai* had the blessing of those in authority. Thanks be to God, that this dark period was short-lived. A repetition of such events must never be allowed in a free Kenya. Yet I must say, I was just beginning to fear that history was about to repeat itself here in Kirinyaga District; that our cry to be protected from evil-doers had gone unheeded. Three weeks ago our Sunday worship was interrupted by two Kanu (party) activists in a move that we saw as highly political; yet no action was taken by the authorities, despite appeals from the Diocesan Synod itself. However, we are very grateful to His Excellency the President for his prompt action in setting up an independent team to investigate the three crimes which have been directed against the Bishop. It is my prayer that the root cause of these problems will be unearthed so that the people of this district can live in peace and tranquillity. I do not fear investigation so long as it is conducted with all fairness. But let all other actors in this drama be investigated also. It was good that the police were quick to apprehend those three leaders who alleged that they knew of a plot to destroy the Bishop's property. Yet, for justice to be seen to be done, why do the police not also apprehend the gentleman who told the whole country that he had proof that the Bishop was having secret meetings with an assistant minister! As far as I am concerned that is a much more serious offence, for it involves the security of the country. To leave such a person at large while the others are languishing in police cells makes people wonder whether this is not a double standard of justice we are practising here in Kirinyaga.Those others who recently issued a statement saying that my utterances are highly subversive, and that my approach is Marxist, should also be apprehended and made to substantiate their allegations. To allege that someone is 'highly subversive and has a Marxist approach' is a more serious charge than to disclose that the Bishop's property might be burned. Let justice take its normal course for all those who make allegations. But to follow only some, and to spare others, may make people wonder whether loyalty to one individual in this district determines what kind of justice is to be exercised. If Kirinyaga District is to enjoy peace, love and unity, these are the areas where 'no stone should be left unturned'. We are grateful to the government for the assurance that (even here in Kirinyaga) 'evil will be punished and good will be encouraged', and that robbery with violence will not be rewarded by promotion but by deserved punishment. We deeply trust that God will soon wipe out the evil in our midst. It cannot last for much longer. And as Christians, our greatest weapon against evil is prayer. So let us continue to pray.

Co-existence and Dialogue

It's my humble appeal to the people of Kirinyaga to stop this habit of isolating some leaders and hurling threats of every kind at them. And I want to tell you that threats will neither frighten nor silence me. With the support and prayers of Christians both here and everywhere in Kenya and the world at large, I will continue to proclaim the Good News of Jesus Christ. Anyone impatient with me should know that I will be around as Diocesan Bishop until the year 2002, unless the Lord himself relieves me earlier. Therefore, let us reason together; let us dialogue. We need to seek reconciliation; and for that to be possible, there has to be a great show of respect for one another. For our part, we are ready to respect party leaders and our political and administrative leaders in this district. We expect them also to reciprocate that respect. But note that we do not seek respect because of who we are, but because of the position we hold in society. Any attempt to isolate the Bishop from his flock would be completely futile. The Christians throughout this Diocese and throughout Kenya are fervently praying for the Bishop and for the faithful during this trying time. Should the politicians in the district wish to perpetuate a cold war, they may do so. But as for us, we shall remain unshaken, because God is on our side. Let these words of Paul to the Ephesians be of special encouragement to all of us:

> Finally, be strong in the Lord and in the strength of his might. Put on the whole armour of God, that you may be able to withstand the wiles of the devil. For we are not contending against flesh and blood, but against the principalities, against the powers, against the world rulers of this present darkness, against the spiritual hosts of wickedness in the heavenly places. Therefore, take the whole armour of God, that you may be able to withstand in the evil day, and having done all to stand. Stand therefore, having girded your loins with the truth, having put on the breastplate of righteousness, and having shod your feet with the equipment of the

gospel of peace; above all taking the shield of faith, with which you can quench all the flaming darts of the evil one. And take the helmet of salvation, and the sword of the Spirit, which is the word of God. Pray at all times in the Spirit, with all prayer and supplication. To that end, keep alert with all perseverance, making supplication for all the saints, and also for me, in opening my mouth boldly to proclaim the mystery of the gospel, for which I am an ambassador in chains, that I may declare it boldly as I ought to speak [Eph. 6:10–20].

Elsewhere Paul had this to say:

'First of all I urge that prayers and supplications, intercessions and thanksgiving be made for all men, for kings and all who are in high positions, that we may lead a quiet and peaceable life, godly and respectable in every way. This is good and is acceptable in the eyes of God our Saviour who desires all men to be saved and to come to know the truth' [1 Tim. 2:1–4].

Amen.

15

Season For Seeking Advice

1 Kings 12

Sermon preached during the inauguration ceremony of the Diocese of Kirinyaga on 2nd September 1990 at St Thomas' Cathedral, Kerugoya.

1. Rehoboam went to Shechem where all the people of northern Israel had gathered to make him king. 2. When Jeroboam Son of Nebat, who had gone to Egypt to escape from King Solomon heard this news, he returned from Egypt. 3. The people of the northern kingdom sent for him, and then they all went together to Rehoboam and said to him, 4. 'Your father Solomon treated us badly and placed heavy burdens on us. If you make these burdens lighter and make life easier for us, we will be your loyal subjects.' 5. 'Come back in three days and I will give you my answer' he replied, and so they left. 6. King Rehoboam consulted the older men who had served as his father Solomon's advisors. 'What answer do you advise me to give these people?' he asked. 7. They replied, 'If you want to serve this people well, give a favourable answer to their request and they will serve you loyally.' 8. But he ignored the advice of the older men and went instead to the young men who had grown up with him, and who were now his advisors. 9. 'What do you advise me to do?' he asked. 'What shall I say to the people who are asking me to make their burdens lighter?' 10. They replied, 'This is what you should tell them, "My little finger is thicker than my father's waist!" 11. Tell them, "My father placed heavy burdens on you; I will make them even heavier. He beat you with whips, I will flog you with bullwhips!" ' 12. Three days later Jeroboam and all the people returned to Rehoboam as he had instructed them. 13. The king ignored the advice of the older men and spoke harshly to the people, as the younger men had advised. 14. He said, 'My father placed heavy burdens on you, I will make them even heavier. He beat you with whips, I will flog you with bullwhips!' 15. It was the will of the Lord to bring about what he had spoken to Jeroboam son of Nebat through the Prophet Ahijah from Shiloh. This is why the king did not pay any attention to the people. 16. When the people saw that the king would not listen to them, they shouted, 'Down with David and his family! What have they ever done for us? Men of Israel, let us go home! Let Rehoboam look out for himself!' 17. So the people of Israel rebelled, leaving Rehoboam as king only of the people who lived in the territory of Judah. 18. Then King Rehoboam sent Adoniram who was in charge of the forced labour to go to the Israelites, but they stoned him to death. At this, Rehoboam hurriedly got in his chariot and escaped to Jerusalem. 19. Ever since that time the people of the northern kingdom of Israel have been in rebellion against the dynasty of David. 20. When the people of Israel heard that Jeroboam had returned from Egypt, they invited him to a meeting of the people and made him king of Israel. Only the tribe of Judah remained royal to David's descendants.

THE SERMON

Seeking advice from other people is certainly an important thing in our bid to succeed in life. School leavers need the advice of teachers and parents with regard to their future careers. A person about to get married needs the advice of older people. And if you are building a new house, you need the advice of others who have built themselves good houses. When we started the Diocese of Mt Kenya East, we invited CORAT (Africa) to advise us on how we could embark on a Community Health Programme, Agriculture, Education etc.

The newly appointed Bishop of Nakuru, the Rt Rev Stephen Njihia, visited us recently, seeking advice on a number of issues. And as we start our new Diocese of Kirinyaga, we would like to be profitably advised, not only by experts but also by ordinary people. Whenever you stand in need of advice, you are likely to get very many advisors. But, as it is said, 'Too many cooks spoil the broth.' Likewise, too many advisors can adversely affect progress unless they speak the same 'language'. I am reminded of that story of an old man, his son, and their donkey, all of whom were headed for the market. On the way they encountered three advisors: The first said, 'Hey, old man! Why don't you let your son ride on the donkey? He looks so tired.' And so the man lifted his son onto the donkey. The second advisor said, 'Hey, young man! How can you be riding on the donkey alone while your old father looks so exhausted from much walking; Old man get onto the donkey also.' The advice was heeded. But the third advisor said, 'Hey look! Two people riding on a poor tired donkey! It is a shame. You should consider carrying it this time for it to have some rest too!' The old man and his son heeded the advice. They tied the donkey's legs, passed a pole through them, and together they carried the donkey upside down. Along the way children laughed and jeered while many others watched in amusement and disbelief. And as the father and son were crossing a river, the panicky donkey could stand it no more. It shook itself away, fell into the river and drowned.

Rehoboam Seeks Advice

When King Solomon died, his son Rehoboam succeeded him as king. Rehoboam travelled from Jerusalem to Shechem to be crowned as king. Note that it was at Shechem that Abraham had built an altar to the Lord; and it was also at Shechem that Joshua had led the children of Israel in a Covenant Renewal. So then, it was in this ancient place of gathering that the ten northern tribes met to make Rehoboam their king. Thousands of people assembled at Shechem to crown their king. But before they could proceed, they needed some assurance. And so they told the king: 'Your father put a heavy yoke on us, but now lighten the harsh and the heavy yoke he put on us, and we will serve you' (1 Ki. 12:4).

The people were humbly requesting the king to lighten the burdens that his father Solomon had laid on the people. King Solomon had made great achievements and is said to have excelled all the kings of the earth in riches and wisdom (1 Ki. 4:20–25). He had completed a 20-year-old building programme, namely: 1. The construction of the temple (7 years). 2. A palace complex (13 years) consisting of Government buildings, the king's house and a house for the Queen of Egypt. 3. He also built chariot offices and the fortification of Meggido and Gezer. 4. He also built a sea port and refinery at the Gulf of Aqaba.

But Solomon carried out his building programme and expansion through harsh measures of exploitation. To pay his tremendous costs he divided his kingdom into tax districts, each with an officer nominated by the king. The real purpose of this administrative reorganization was to centralize power in the crown by replacing the old tribal system with twelve districts under the supervision of the local nominees, two of whom were Solomon's sons-in-law. Equally oppressive was Solomon's programme of forced labour. 30,000 Israelites were conscripted and sent off to labour camps in Lebanon for one month out of every three (1 Ki. 5:13–18). They felled the great cedars of Lebanon, floated them down the Phoenician Coast to Joppa and then carried them over the hills to Jerusalem. 80,000 Israelites were put to work in the stone quarries, while 70,000 others toiled as burden bearers. Hence Solomon's building programme meant heavy burdens and exploitation of the people. But the people themselves had demanded the institution of the king and took no heed when the prophet Samuel warned them: 'If you want a king like the oriental monarchs, then you must reckon with a danger that his power will limit your liberties, secularize your outlook and undermine the very foundations of the Covenant Community.'

The ten northern tribes had begun to grumble long before Solomon's death. The prospects of another king of Solomon's type certainly spelt doom and hence their firm request to king Rehoboam. But he did not rush to answer the people. This was wisdom at work! He told the people to 'go away for three days and then come back to me' [1 Ki. 12:5]. In sending away the people, the king wanted to have enough time to consult his advisors so as to give an answer to the people.

The Advice of Elders

King Rehoboam consulted the elders who had served his father Solomon during his lifetime. The advice of the elders was as follows: 'If today you will be a servant of these people and serve them and give them a favourable answer, they will be your servants' [1 Ki. 12:7]. The elders who had worked with Solomon, and who knew what had gone wrong, advised Rehoboam to be a 'servant of the people, not their master'. They advised him to remove the burdens which Solomon had laid on the people.

The Advice of the Peer Group

Rehoboam rejected the advice of the elders because they told him what he was not wanting to hear. He then went to his own peer group – to the men who had grown up with him and asked them, 'What is your advice? How should we answer these people who say that I should lighten the yoke that my father Solomon put on them?' [1 Ki. 12:9] And the young people replied: 'Tell these people, "My little finger is thicker than my father's waist; my father laid on you a heavy yoke, and I will make it even heavier." ' (v. 10–11). 'My father scourged you with whips, I will scourge you with scorpions' (v. 11b).

Three days later, the people turned up at Shechem in their thousands to hear the King's reply. The king went up to the platform and he answered the people harshly, having rejected the elders' advice and taken that of the youth [v. 14].

Consequences

When all Israel saw that the king refused to listen to them they answered the king: 'What share do we have in David? What part in Jesse's son? To your tents O Israel. Look after your own house, O David!' (v. 16). We are told that the king sent out Adoniram who was in charge of the forced labour, probably to cool the people down, but they stoned him to death. And so on that day, Israel rebelled against the house of David and the kingdom was divided into two – the northern kingdom under Jeroboam and the southern kingdom under Rehoboam.

Season for Seeking Advice From the People

The Kenya Government has done something that has never happened before. The government and the party have decided to seek advice from Kenyans of all walks of life, on 'The Kenya we Want'. The Kanu Review Committee, chaired by the Vice President the Hon. George Saitoti, and composed of selected men and women, has gone round the country listening to what people are saying about the future of their country. At one time the House of Bishops suggested that a National Convention be called to discuss the same subject. But surely such a convention could be attended only by the educated and the wealthy. But in the case of the Kanu Review Committee, the ordinary *Wananchi* have been given a chance to advise the Party and the Government. Personally I was at Nyeri to present the Memoranda of the Diocese of Kirinyaga. I was surprised to find that the people who had turned up were ordinary people – peasant farmers, some dressed quite shoddily with torn clothes. They had anxiously turned up to make use of this golden opportunity of a lifetime, to air their own views for the betterment of their government and the only party. Now the government and the party have heard and it is up to them to choose what advice they will follow. The future peace and stability of this country may depend on the kind of advice those in authority will heed. Rehoboam rejected the wise counsel of the elders and chose to follow the misleading advice of his contemporaries. Kenyans are not really asking for the removal of big burdens; indeed, compared to some of our neighbouring countries, Kenya is far better in many ways. However, we believe it could be better still and it is because of this that Kenyans are humbly requesting the following, as a means of greater peace and prosperity in the land.

No More Rigging of Elections

We fought for independence so that we can elect leaders of our own choice through the 'One person One Vote' principle. The imposition of unpopular leaders by allowing people who receive fewer votes to be declared winners makes a mockery of democracy. Democracy is not the rule of politicians by politicians and for politicians but the rule of the people by the people and for the people.

People are saying No! to the *mlolongo* (Queuing) method of voting. People are saying, No! to expulsion of people from Kanu; they are demanding that those who have been expelled be reinstated and be allowed to participate fully in free and fair elections.

People are saying No! to the practice of detaining people without a fair trial in a court of law. 'Let justice be done and be seen to have been done.' When three politicians said in April 1989 that they had discovered a plot to damage my property, they were arrested and taken to the prison in Nyeri for a month and then ordered to report at the Police Station weekly. Yet when an assistant chief grabs a microphone from Bishop Muge (at Immanuel Church Mutira in 1988), or when politicians threaten bishops with death, they are not arrested and charged: hence people are saying No! to the apparent practice of a double standard of justice.

People are saying, 'Let no stone be left unturned until all murderers are arrested, charged and punished.' No stones, including the very heavy ones, should be left unturned. But it seems that some stones are too heavy to be turned and so murderers are left unpunished.

People are saying, 'Peace, love and unity are wonderful slogans, but let justice be our shield and defender, because there is no way that these three can thrive without the presence of justice.'

People are saying, 'Let the coffee farmers receive a fair reward for their labour.'

People are saying, 'Let there be no more harassment of lawyers and no more harrassment of hawkers. Let there be no more *Muoroto*[1] incidents.'

The Saitoti Committee has given people the courage to speak for themselves and that is how it should be. In the recent past, people were looking up to the bishops to speak for them and it was said 'Let the Bishop Speak'[2] Now it is the people's turn. Let the people speak! May the Saitoti Review Committee sort out all the advice they have been given and may they have the wisdom and courage to make recommendations which will truly give us the Kenya we want, for the sake of the peace, stability and prosperity of our nation. Amen.

1. Muoroto is the name of a roadside squatter community in Nairobi, that was destroyed by city council bulldozers one early morning while the people slept. A number of people inside the community were killed.
2. This refers to the remark of President Moi after Bishop Gitari's fiery sermons in 1987 which led to bitter reaction from some politicians. It became the title of the collection of those sermons published by Uzima Press in 1988.

16

Was There No Naboth to Say No?

THE SETTING

The sermon based on 1 Kings 21:1–29, was preached at Trinity Church, Mutuma, near Kamuruana hill in Kirinyaga on 19th May 1991. It followed the allocation of a large part of the hill by the Kirinyaga County Council, to two local politicians posing as JIMKA and JAKEN companies.

The Kamuruana hill is public land of great environmental importance. As such the Bishop (on behalf of the Christians and all people of goodwill in Kirinyaga) expressed great concern that the destruction of the Kamuruana forest would adversely affect the environment and natural beauty of the area.

THE SERMON

One of the most interesting dramas in the Bible is the encounter between King Ahab and a peasant farmer by the name of Naboth. Every drama has actors, and in this particular drama, there were 4 actors: King Ahab, Naboth the peasant farmer, Jezebel the Queen and Elijah the prophet.

The drama developed along the following lines: Naboth, an ordinary man and a neighbour to the king, had a piece of land which he had inherited from his forefathers. The king developed an interest in this piece of land and desired to have it in order to extend his vegetable garden. But Naboth said No!

Ahab the Evil Ruler

King Ahab ruled as the seventh king of the northern kingdom for 22 years from 874 to 852 BC. The writer of 1 Kings thus summarizes the reign of King Ahab: 'Ahab son of Omri did more evil in the eyes of the Lord than any of those before him' (1 Ki. 16:30). Note that the 22 years of the king's reign are remembered more by the evils he did than the good he might have done. Though he built himself a palace and inlaid it with ivory, and though he fortified cities, the Bible dismisses Ahab as a king who did more evil in the eyes of the Lord than any other king before him. There are two aspects of his reign that made him earn the condemnation.

Firstly, he mingled the worship of the living God with the worship of Baal, by marrying Jezebel, the daughter of the king of Sidon, who brought with her the gods of the Sidonians and introduced Baal worship into Israel. A temple to Baal Melgart was built in Samaria (1 Ki. 16:35f) and Jezebel, a strong minded woman, (filled with an almost missionary zeal for her gods) sought to make the cult of Baal the official religion in the King's palace. Ahab, a King of Israel who knew the first commandment, 'Thou shalt have no other gods but me', did not only compromise his religion but was daring enough to allow the worship of the living God to go side by side with the worship of idols.

The importation of a foreign cult (religion) into the land of Yahweh (God), and the predominance it was given in the king's palace through the patronage of queen Jezebel moved the prophet Elijah to challenge King Ahab at Mt Carmel as we read in 1 Kings 18:21. 'How long will you waver between two opinions? If the Lord is God, follow him, but if Baal is God, follow him.' Ahab has been called the most evil king Israel ever had, for allowing the worship of God side by side with the worship of idols. Idolatry has been defined as the worship of a man-made-god instead of worshipping God who created man. This is what Paul Tillich termed as 'being ultimately concerned by that which is not ultimate'. When we put our hope and security in material things, they become our idols but the time comes when we realize that they are of no lasting help. At Mt Carmel Elijah demonstrated the power of the living God by calling fire from heaven in a matter of a few minutes. By contrast, the prophets of Baal prayed to their god from morning till noon. The idol did not answer their prayers because an idol is nothing and is helpless, although it embodies a demonic force that a person of God must reckon with. Christian people everywhere must remember that it does not please the living God if they go to Church on a Sunday to worship God and on Monday start worshipping man-made idols. Christians! Beware of these idols: Money, Wealth, Lies, Guns and Military Strength, Political Power, God-fathers, etc. All idols have one thing in common – they are deceptive, and to put our trust and to seek security in them has disastrous consequences. Our security can be found only in amending our ways and truly executing justice in the land, as the prophet Jeremiah says:

> 'If you truly amend your ways and your doings, if you truly execute justice one with another, if you do not oppress the alien, the fatherless or the widow, or shed innocent blood in this place, and if you do not go after other gods to your own hurt then I will let you dwell in this place, in the place that I gave of old to your fathers for ever' [Jer. 7:5–7]

Ahab's second sin was the oppression of the poor. He had a tendency to enrich himself at the expense of the poor. It is clear that there was great prosperity in Israel. Omri, his father, had bought land to build his new capital in Samaria. The city was began by Omri and was completed by Ahab. Archeologists have shown that the city completed by Ahab had fortifications unequalled in ancient Palestine for excellent workmanship. His palace was decorated with ivory and he lived in great luxury. But the prosperity of the king and his high standard of living was achieved at the expense of the poor people because the system then as now tended to place the poor at the mercy of the rich and the influential. If during difficult times the poor were forced by circumstances to borrow money from the rich, the rich would in turn charge very high interest rates and if they failed to pay in time, they faced either eviction from their land, or slavery.

The story of Naboth and his vineyard is one of the best illustrations of the evils of King Ahab. There are four things that we learn about Naboth:- that Naboth was clearly an ordinary citizen, neither rich nor poor. He was not a man of high rank in society. He was just an ordinary person and a good citizen. Secondly, Naboth had a piece of land in Jezreel. The valley of Jezreel was one of the most fertile parts of Palestine and was agriculturally very valuable. Naboth had already planted grapes on his piece of land. Thirdly, we know that Naboth's vineyard was close to the palace of Ahab the king of Israel. In other words this ordinary peasant farmer was a neighbour to the king. In this neighbourhood, there lived two men who are greatly contrasted; a king and a peasant farmer. Fourthly, Naboth knew his rights as far as land issues were concerned and was prepared to defend these rights fearlessly even if it meant death.

The King Encounters Naboth

One day Ahab approached Naboth with the request, 'Let me have your vineyard; it is close to my palace; and I want to use the land for a vegetable garden. I will give you a better vineyard for it, or if you prefer, I will pay you a fair price' [1 Ki. 21:1–2].

Note that the king himself left his palace and went to visit the home of this peasant farmer to make a humble request. After all, Ahab was not completely bad – he did not send any of his officials, he went in person to make that humble request. It is obviously a great privilege for any citizen to be visited by the king of the land. However, for theological reasons the king's request was unacceptable to Naboth. Naboth replied firmly: 'The Lord forbid that I should give you the inheritance of my fathers' [verse 3]. Even if the terms of the king were generous enough, Naboth refused to sell his land or even to exchange it. There are two reasons why he did this. Firstly, the land was not Naboth's property to dispose of as he pleased; the land belonged to the whole clan and it had been passed down from generation to generation as a sacred inheritance. Secondly, the Israelites believed that the land belonged to God and God gave each family a piece of land so that the family could act as stewards of God's property. The stewards were supposed to administer the land for the welfare of the whole community. It followed that no one had the right to grab land, not even the king himself. This peasant farmer, Naboth, understood the theology of the land and was prepared to re-affirm to the king himself the ancient basis of Israel's land tenure. 'No inheritance in Israel is to pass from tribe to tribe, for every Israelite shall keep the tribal land inherited from his fore-fathers' [Nu. 36:7].

Naboth was therefore convinced that it was not within his power to sell the land to anyone, not even to the king himself, because this would have been a violation of the divine law which forbade a man to alienate any part of the family inheritance. Naboth found himself compelled to choose between pleasing the king and pleasing the King of Kings. There are times when believers are forced to choose between compliance with human law and obedience to the divine law. When Peter and John were ordered by the Sanhedrin (Council of Elders) that under no circumstances were they to speak or to teach in the name of Jesus, Peter and John replied: 'You yourselves judge which is right in God's sight – to obey you or to obey God.

For we cannot stop speaking about what we ourselves have seen and heard' [Acts 4:19–20]. Though we have a duty to render to Caesar what is Caesar's we must say No, to Caesar, if his requests contradict the will of God for his people and his creation. The Law of God is higher than that of human beings. Hence, if we have to make a choice, the inferior law must yield to the higher – loyalty to God takes precedence over all other considerations. Naboth knew clearly that if he had to choose between the king's injustices and the righteousness of God, he had to choose the latter. Hence Naboth said No to the king categorically, whatever the consequences. Naboth took his stand on the written word of God and refused to act contrary to the divine law.

The story of Naboth urges us to seek to know our fundamental human rights and to defend those rights at whatever cost. The story also serves as a warning to all land grabbers, whoever they be. Land is the most precious commodity and we cannot be mere spectators watching a few rich people and politicians grab as much land as they want, to extend their 'vegetable gardens'.

Stewardship of Land

The County Council of Kirinyaga has the duty to exercise good stewardship of land entrusted to it for the benefit of all people. On 19th February 1991, the County Council of Kirinyaga Ordinary Works, Town Planning, Markets and Housing Committee met in the Council's Committee room. The meeting began at 11.35 am with prayers. According to Minute 37/91 of that meeting the Council Chairman tabled an application letter from Kariko Jaken Tree Nurseries in which they requested the Council to allocate a twenty-acre plot for the Establishment of a Tree Nursery at Kamuruana Hill.

In the short discussion which ensued, members felt that a Tree Nursery at the hill was ideal for the local residents and the District at large but recommended ten acres instead of twenty acres. It was thereupon agreed, 'that a ten-acre plot for establishment of a tree nursery at Kamuruana hill be allocated to M/S Kariko Jaken Tree Nurseries'. There was not a single Naboth with courage to say No!

Min. 39/91: An application for a motel site at Kamuruana Hill by M/S Jimka Developers and Lodges Company was considered and approved. Of the 16 Councillors who met, there was not a single one with the courage of Naboth, to say No! There are two main reasons why Kamuruana hill should not be given to either 'Jaken' or 'Jimka' to extend their 'Vegetable gardens', or for any other purpose. Firstly, Kamuruana hill must be preserved and protected for environmental reasons. The people who live around this hill have noted that since the beautiful forest which covered the hill was cut in 1987, the climate around the hill has been greatly affected. The hill used to be covered with clouds but now the clouds have moved into the forest. Clearing the trees without immediately replanting more trees has left the hill naked and it has thus lost its traditional beauty. The nakedness of this hill reminds me of the words of St Paul in Romans 8:19:

> The creation waits with eager expectation for the sons of God to be revealed. For the creation was subjected to frustration not by its own choice . . . that the creation itself will be liberated from its bondage to decay and brought into the glorious

freedom of the children of God. We know that the whole creation has been groaning as in the pains of child-birth, right up to the present time.

When God created Adam and Eve he gave them authority over all creation. Their mandate however, was to cultivate the earth responsibly, not to exploit it irresponsibly. Kamuruana hill is groaning with pain at its nakedness.

The hill was not created for JAKEN and JIMKA to extend their 'vegetable gardens' – it was created for all of us to enjoy its beauty and its environment. One of the recommendations of the Kanu Review Committee reads: 'That the Kanu Constitution should be amended to provide that the preservation and protection of the environment will be one of the objectives of the party' (page 118 of the Saitoti Report, Sec. 3, part B, No 8.10.13). To the best of my knowledge, that recommendation was adopted by the Delegates Conference held at Kasarani, Nairobi in December 1990 and should be respected by our County Council. Moreover, the Kirinyaga District Development Committee meeting at Kerugoya in August last year resolved that Murinduko Hill, Kamuruana Hill and Njukiini Forest should be preserved and protected for environmental purposes.

Secondly, if the County Council of Kirinyaga has land it wishes to lease out, then surely it should not be given to people who have already grabbed many acres and plots of land, but should first and foremost be given to the desperately poor and landless people living in our midst. Only a short distance from here, near Kangaita Tea Factory, there are sixteen families living temporarily on a short section of the road. These seventy-seven people were removed from Nyagithuci Forest just above Kangaita. I visited the Community the other day and they look harassed and helpless and without hope. There are many such people throughout the district. While it is true that landlessness will always be a problem because of the increase of population, land entrusted to the County Council should not be left at the mercy of greedy land-grabbers when it can ease the problem of poverty. We call upon the leaders of Kirinyaga and especially the Councillors to review the following issues which are of great concern to the people they are supposed to represent: 1. Improvement of Kamuruana environment through replanting of trees and by saying 'No' to any unscrupulous 'Jimka' or 'Jaken'. If necessary, the Diocese of Kirinyaga is prepared to participate in this noble cause by mobilizing its youth in the replanting of trees on the hill. 2. As a matter of principle, all public land reserved for public utilities should not be interfered with and should be distributed for public utilities such as: schools, Churches, recreation – public parks, football fields, social halls, childrens play-grounds and cemeteries.

First Cardinal Principle

It is the duty of the County Council and the Municipal Council to ensure that any land preserved for public utility is not interfered with. However, the County Council, and to some extent the Municipal Council, seem to have different ideas about such public land.

For instance, the 140 acres of cattle-holding ground at Sagana have been converted to other uses. We have information that one powerful individual has grabbed 60 acres of that land for his own use and some of his supporters have also received a share of this public land. And there was no Naboth to say 'No!'

A plot reserved for a social hall at Kianyaga was sub-divided 4 times – the social hall was demolished and although another site was allocated, only the foundation has been constructed. The people of Kianyaga have no Social Hall. And there was no Naboth to say 'No' to the demolition.

It is alleged that a piece of land reserved for a cemetery at Kagio has been given to an individual to build a shop, and there was no Naboth to say 'No!'

A few individuals have been given 5 acres belonging to Wang'uru Secondary School and they have allegedly cut the school fence and started cultivating the land, and there was no Naboth to say 'No!'.

What about a leader in Mwea who is grabbing valuable public land in and around Ngurubani township, yet there is no Naboth to say 'No!'?

There are allegations that land reserved as a public park at Kutus where children can play and people take a walk in open surroundings has also been given away to an individual, and there was no Naboth to say 'No!'.

Second Cardinal Principle

When the Council or the Municipality acquires land from individuals or families for public utilities etc, there should be no delay in compensating those individuals with alternative land and proper (and) legal procedures of land transfer should be carried out without unnecessary delay. But the situation now is that some people have been given alternative land while still holding Title Deeds to the original land and as a result powerful land-grabbers have come to bargain with them so that they can keep part of that land and surrender the larger part to the unscrupulous bidder. This is how the land acquired for extension of the Kerugoya/Kutus Municipality and other urban and shopping centres has been lost to a few rich men. Not long ago, at Kutus township, the Kerugoya/Kutus Municipal Council compulsorily acquired land from a number of people in order to provide public utilities in the township. These people were compensated with land elsewhere by the County Council, but for unknown reasons, about 50 acres now belong to one or two powerful politicians who are busy fencing them. And there was no Naboth to say 'No!'.

Third Cardinal Principle

Individuals who apply for plots should pay the legal fees to the Council itself. But it is alleged that in some cases all that you need to do is to give one individual Ksh 30,000/- and you get the plot. As a result, some people have become millionaires overnight by harvesting where they did not plant, and there is no Naboth to say 'No!'.

Fourth Cardinal Principle

Anyone who is given free land by the County Council or the Municipal Council to undertake any kind of development should be monitored to ensure that he undertakes the development for which he was given the land. But now the common practice is that people are given land that was compulsorily acquired for use by the Council. Immediately they are given two acres, they sub-divide the land into small plots and then sell them at exorbitant prices, thus harvesting where they did not plant. If such land has to be sold, the right people to sell it would be the original owners or the County Council itself. It is most likely that if 'Jaken' is given the ten acres, he will not put up a Tree Nursery. He is likely to sub-divide it and sell it to individuals for a lot of money.

Fifth Cardinal Principle

If the County Council has property it wishes to dispose of, such as old vehicles and tractors, the sale of this property should be advertized and the general public invited to tender, in which case the highest bidder should buy the property. Sometime ago, the council's tractor and trailer was bought by one individual at a throw-away price!

Sixth Cardinal Principle

Elected leaders and top civil servants should not be the main beneficiaries of the land entrusted to the Council. They were elected not to grab land but to care for the poor and the landless. How is it that a number of past District Commissioners now own acres and acres in our district, given to them freely by the Kirinyaga County Council, when many landless families are in village plots and cultivate along the roadside? And there was no Naboth to say 'No!'. My greatest worry about the rigging of elections is that when people go to Parliament or County Council by selection rather than election, they cease to be concerned with the welfare of the people and are more concerned to please the godfathers who helped them to get their present positions of power. For instance if 'Jimka' helped to ensure the election of some councillors to the Council, there is no way they can have the courage to say 'No', to his wicked intentions of grabbing Kamuruana Hill because they are already mortgaged. But I want to say this, if the councillors are no longer capable of saying 'No' to land grabbers then they have outlived their usefulness and may as well call it a day!

When Naboth said 'No' to King Ahab, we read that the king went home depressed and angry. He lay down on his bed, facing the wall, and would not eat. But the story did not end there. Jezebel the wife of the king came and found him resting on the bed and looking miserable because Naboth had refused to comply with his wishes. She asked him, 'Is this how you act as a king? Get up and eat – cheer up. I will get you the vineyard of Naboth the Jezreelite.'

At her instruction, Naboth was charged with two serious crimes by two 'good for nothing' people. He was accused of cursing God and the king. In other words he was accused of blasphemy and treason. Unfortunately, Naboth was not given any opportunity to defend himself or even to have access to a lawyer. Jezebel wrote letters in Ahab's name and sealed them. She then sent them to the elders and nobles living in Naboth's city, ordering that Naboth be stoned to death. The elders and nobles did not bother to scrutinize the authenticity of the letters, otherwise they would have discovered they were a forgery; and so they simply followed the orders from 'above'. We see too much injustice being practised by those who claim to have received orders from 'above'. Not long ago in this district there was a headmistress who was given only a few hours to clear out of the school, allegedly with orders from 'above'. And in the same way the chairman of that school whom we considered able and quite dedicated was also replaced without any consultation with the sponsor. Refusal to allow Naboth to defend himself meant that justice was not done, neither was it seen to have been done. Naboth was accused by professional liars who were bribed to tell lies against him. When Naboth was put to death, Jezebel said to Ahab, 'Naboth is dead, now go and take possession of the vineyard which he refused to sell to you.' So Ahab went and took possession of the vineyard and must have started fencing it off. But the story did not end there. The prophet Elijah was commanded by God to go down and confront King Ahab. In an earlier story when Elijah emerged from hiding, King Ahab greeted him with the words: 'Is that you, you troubler of Israel?' [1 Ki. 18:17]. That greeting poses a big question. Who is the troubler of Israel? Elijah or Ahab? Prophet Micah thus described the trouble makers of his day:

> How terrible it will be for those who lie awake and plan evil! When the morning comes as soon as they have the chance, they do the evil they planned. When they want fields they seize them. When they want houses they take them. No man's family or property is safe! [Mic. 2:1–2].

Who are the troublers in Kenya? They are the land-grabbers, the election riggers, the councillors who sit and participate in wrong decision-making and lack the courage to say 'No!'. The troublers of Kenya are those who wish to put the clock back so that we can revert to *mlolongo* (queueing) method of elections. The troublers of Kenya are those who plan unwarranted transfers of civil servants, who do not support them politically, thus causing suffering to innocent students. The troublers of Kenya are those who organize thuggery and raiding of people's homes at night. They are those who refuse to improve our human rights record so that justice can be our shield and defender! They sing 'Peace, peace', when there is no peace. And Elijah, standing before Ahab after Naboth's death said to him:

> You have devoted yourself completely to doing what is wrong in the Lord's sight, so the Lord says to you, 'I will bring disaster on you. I will do away with you and get rid of every male in your family young or old alike. Your family will become like the family of King Jeroboam. . . . Because you have stirred up my anger by leading Israel into sin' [18:20–22].

When Elijah had finished speaking, Ahab tore his clothes, put them off and wore sack-cloth. He refused food, slept in the sack-cloth and went about gloomy and depressed. The Lord said to Elijah,

> Have you noticed how Ahab has humbled himself before me? Since he has done this I will not bring disaster on him during his lifetime. It will be during his son's life time that I will bring disaster on Ahab's family [18:29].

A Forgiving God

The character of our God is that he is a forgiving God. Even if Ahab had done more evil than any other king before him, God was willing to forgive him. But

God could forgive him only because of his willingness to humble himself before God and to repent of his sins. The Bible says that we have all sinned and come short of the glory of God. And the Prayer Book says, 'If we say we have no sins we deceive ourselves and the truth is not in us. But if we confess our sins he is merciful and willing to forgive us all our unrighteousness'. We should not think it is only those who have given Kamuruana hill away who have sinned. We have all sinned because we have created an atmosphere which allows such things to happen. We should be remorseful for those things which we ought to have done and we have not done; and also for those things we have done which we ought not to have done. In other words we should repent of both our sins of omission and sins of commission. If we truly repent and do not repeat those evil things, God in his mercy will forgive us. This was the very purpose for which Jesus died. Indeed he is telling us:

> Come to me, all of you who are tired from carrying heavy loads and I will give you rest. Take my yoke and put it on you, and learn from me, because I am gentle and humble in spirit and you will find rest. For the yoke I will give you is easy and the load I will put on you is light. [Mt. 11:28–30]. Amen.

17

You are Doomed, You Shepherds of Israel

Ezekiel 34

Sermon preached at St. Thomas' Church, Kerugoya on 9th June 1991

THE SERMON

The image of a leader as a shepherd occurs about eleven times in the Old Testament and about six times in the New Testament. The whole of Ezekiel chapter 34 is devoted to this important image of a leader as a shepherd. Many of you here are in positions of leadership and for that reason I beg that you read this passage as though it is directed to you. The message therein is relevant for teachers and heads of schools, for chairmen of farmers' co-operatives, village and market leaders, assistant chiefs, District Officers, District Commissioners, Provincial Commissioners and even the Head of State, and many more.

Ezekiel begins his prophecy by asserting that it is the Lord who has spoken to him, commanding him to 'denounce the rulers of Israel' and to tell them what 'I, the sovereign Lord say to them: "You are doomed, you shepherds of Israel. You are doomed." ' There are a number of reasons why Ezekiel told the leaders that they were doomed. The main reason was that they were not looking after the sheep properly. He says: 'You take care of yourselves but never tend the sheep (verse 2). You drink the milk, wear clothes made from the wool and kill and eat the finest sheep (verse 3). You have not taken care of the weak ones: you have not healed those that are sick; you have not bandaged those that are hurt; you have not brought back those that wander off; you have not looked for those that are lost (verse 4). Instead you have treated them cruelly.' There are two broad categories of sin: sins of commission and sins of omission. The sin of commission is when you do that which you ought not do, while the sin of omission is when you fail to do that which you ought to have done. The leaders of Israel were doomed for the following sins of commission:

Taking care of themselves and forgetting the sheep;
Milking the sheep, killing and eating the finest;
Treating the sheep cruelly.

And the following were the sins of omission:

Failure to heal the sick;
Failure to bandage those that are hurt;
Failure to look for the lost and bring them back to the fold.

A good shepherd is one who thinks more about the sheep than himself or herself. The good shepherd cares for the sheep; when they are hungry he feeds them, and when they thirst he gives them water, when they are hurt he dresses the wounds, and when they are sick he provides healing. A good shepherd looks for the lost sheep and brings them back to the fold. He protects the flock against thieves and wild animals. When there is danger, the good shepherd does not run away; he would rather die for the flock.

The shepherds of Israel were doomed first and foremost because they cared for themselves more than they did for the sheep which then wandered away aimlessly, becoming victims of wild animals and thieves.

The leaders in Kenya today are no different from the leaders of Israel in the days of the prophet Ezekiel. We are grateful to the press which keeps us up-to-date with news of how our leaders are succeeding in caring for themselves.

On Friday, June 7th 1991 the *Standard* in a banner story gave us names of people owing the Kenya Grain Growers Co-operative Union (KGGCU) millions of shillings. This is not little money! I wonder whether you know that it is less than a million days since Jesus Christ was born. 1991 × 365 = 726,715 days. We still have another 273,285 days (or 748 years) to reach a million days since Christ! But some of our leaders owe millions of shillings. Over 35 million shillings is owed KGGCU by people in the government:

Minister of Energy	13,000,000
Minister of Livestock Development	3,500,000
Minister for Local Government	3,700,000
Minister for Research, Science & Technology	3,000,000
A Nominated Member of Parliament	7,000,000
Former Assistant Minister for Agriculture	4,000,000

These people are owing so many millions of shillings while KGGCU is going down through financial strain. When leaders borrow money from such an organization and do not pay in time, someone is suffering somewhere, and that is the farmer. Eventually the farmers' organization might find itself unable to serve *wananchi* (citizens) adequately.

The same can be said of African leaders who keep millions of dollars in foreign banks so that when the day of reckoning comes and they have to run away, they can live comfortably with the money they milked from the flock they were meant to care for.

Nearer home, we have leaders whose main preoccupation is to grab land while the future of thousands of landless poor families is yet to be determined. In Kutus township, land which was compulsorily taken away from its owners (in 1972) for purposes of providing public utilities was in 1989 grabbed by a few leaders who are now busy sub-dividing and selling it at exorbitant prices. It is said that one of these leaders and his wife have as much as 34 acres, not to mention the ground for 60 cattle that they grabbed at Sagana. The open park opposite the Kenya Commercial Bank in Kerugoya town has also been grabbed and unless serious efforts are made to reverse this evil trend, we may end up by having no open place for free relaxation.

On 19th May 1991, thousands of worshippers expressed solidarity with the Bishop in his protest against Kamuruana hill being allocated to JIMKA and JAKEN private developers for the extension of their 'vegetable gardens'. I want, on your behalf and that of the people of Kirinyaga, to thank the District Commissioner for assuring the public that Kamuruana hill will remain intact and that it will be preserved for environmental purposes. We are also grateful that the university students planted some trees there yesterday. Yet in spite of all these positive signs, it is still a matter of great concern that the full meeting of Kirinyaga County Council held on Tuesday 28th May, passed a resolution that JIMKA should be given 2 acres at the hilltop to build a motel, and JAKEN be given 10 acres for a tree nursery. But, as I said at Mutuma, 'Kamuruana hill was not created for JIMKA and JAKEN to extend their "vegetable gardens;" it is for all of us to enjoy its beauty and environment.'

The County Council of Kirinyaga must not underestimate the intelligence of Kirinyaga people. If the Council dares to go ahead and allocate the hill to JIMKA and JAKEN, that very act and many other acts of land grabbing will cost them their votes at the next general elections, for the people of Kirinyaga cannot afford to elect to the council self-seeking leaders who are not at all concerned about the feelings and the welfare of the electorate.

Ezekiel laments, 'Shepherds of Israel, you are doomed . . .'; and now he says to the shepherds of Kirinyaga, 'You are doomed. You care for yourselves but never tend the sheep.'

The shepherds of Israel were accused of drinking the milk, wearing clothes made from the sheep's wool and eating the finest sheep. In other words, the shepherds only exploited the sheep and never really tended them. The sheep were important as long as they could gratify the greedy desires of the shepherds. We know exactly what Ezekiel would say if he were around today to witness the harsh manner in which the government is handling the hawkers of Muoroto and other parts of the city, not to mention the recent demolition of kiosks in Chuka town.

There is a disgusting story of a leader in this district who happens to be a lawyer, and whose sister-in-law had an accident sometime ago from which she became paralyzed. The learned friend offered to negotiate compensation with the insurance company and settled for 600,000 shillings which was actually too little for a person paralyzed for life. The learned friend gave the girl only 200,000 shillings and pocketed the rest. The girl had to hire another lawyer to help to recover the balance. 'You are doomed, you shepherds of Kirinyaga'! reverberates the words of Ezekiel.

What about those shepherds who are supposed to care for the people detained without trial? According to Edith, wife of the detained Kenneth Matiba, her husband suffered a stroke on the night of 25/26 May 1991 in the lone cell block, as a result of which a vein ruptured and bled into his brain. But for eight full days the authorities would only administer pain killers instead of rushing him to the hospital. Even when they finally took him to hospital for a C.T. scan, they rushed him back to his lone cell until his condition worsened, when again he was taken to the hospital. They would not even allow his wife to see him until after several days. This negligence reminds us how the late Steve Bantu Biko was handled by South African racist authorities in 1977. What a shame!

In a nation whose national anthem starts with 'O God of all creation, bless this our land and nation.' such negligence must not be tolerated. We call upon the government to release the sick Matiba on humanitarian grounds so that his family can make the necessary arrangements for specialized treatment overseas. 'You are doomed you prison authorities, you have not healed those that are sick, bandaged those that are hurt; rather, you have treated them cruelly'.

What about the unfair tax the county council has started imposing on women traders in the open market, and the subsequent confiscation of goods of those who cannot afford to pay it. You are doomed! says the prophet of God.

The Sheep are not Blameless

In verses 17 to 25 of the same chapter, the sovereign Lord analyzes the characteristics of the sheep. He says to them: 'You are not satisfied with eating the best grass; you even trample down what you do not eat. You drink clear water and then you make muddy what you do not drink. You push the sick ones aside and butt them away from the flock.'

In other words the sheep are accused of selfishness. Even when the good shepherd takes them to the best grass, they eat and then start spoiling what they do not eat. As a result of all this the Lord will judge the sheep and will separate the good from the bad and the sheep from the goats. The Lord God will judge between the strong sheep and the weak sheep.

The Good Shepherd

Because of the negligence of the shepherds the sheep were attacked by wild animals. And so the Lord says to the shepherds: 'I the sovereign Lord declare that I am your enemy. I will take the sheep away from you, never again to let you be their shepherd. I will rescue my sheep from you and not let you eat them.'

How wonderful it is to know that God cannot leave his sheep to be exploited forever, because the sheep belong to him. He appoints leaders to be his stewards but how miserably often do they fail! When the good shepherd takes the sheep away from the exploiters he will demonstrate the true qualities of a good shepherd. He will look for the sheep and care for them (v. 11). He will look for the scattered sheep and bring them back to the fold; he will search for them wherever they might be, (including those that have run away to foreign lands). He will gather them together back to their own land (v. 13). He will feed them in pleasant pastures. He will destroy the fat and the strong and get rid of all the dangerous animals in the land so that the sheep can graze safely in the fields and sleep peacefully . . . .

And now I suggest that you read on from the scriptures and get the thrilling beauty of the analysis of the Good Shepherd. God bless you!

Immediately after the sermon, someone brought the news that on the KBC 1 o'clock news bulletin it had been announced that Mr Kenneth Matiba[1] *had just been released. The Bishop informed the congregation and there was great rejoicing. The Bishop then led in prayers of thanksgiving for Matiba's release.*

1. Mr Kenneth Matiba was detained during the famous *Saba Saba* (i.e 7/7/90) for openly campaigning for the re-introduction of multi-party politics in Kenya. Widespread riots had occurred in parts of the city and the neighbouring districts. Several innocent people, including school children, were reportedly killed in the fracas when the notorious General Service Unit was let loose by the Police Commissioner following orders by the President to 'do everything possible to control the situation'.

18

The Tower of Babel

Genesis 11:1–9

THE SERMON

The story of Noah and the flood is well known even from our Sunday School days. After the flood we read how God blessed Noah and his sons, saying to them: 'Be fruitful and multiply and fill the earth.' But when they came to the land of Shinar and settled there they had a different idea. 'Let us build ourselves a city . . .' they said to one another. It appears that the sons of men did not agree with the idea of spreading and scattering all over the earth. They thought they would be happier and safer if they kept together. By so doing they thought they were cleverer than either God or Noah. There were two things which gave them an advantage in remaining together:

1. Language: They had one language and so they understood one another. By building a city for themselves, they intended to form a more cohesive society where everybody spoke one language, and where everybody showed caring love and support for the other.
2. Land: The people had found a very convenient and spacious land in which to settle – a plain in the land of Shinar which was large and fertile and which they thought would support the entire population.

The people were unanimous in their resolve to build a city and a tower that reached the heavens. They did not seek God's will at all. Note how they excited and encouraged one another to set about the work: 'Come, let us make bricks and burn them thoroughly. Come, let us build ourselves a city' [vv 3, 4]. By mutual encouragement they made one another more daring and resolute.

Motives For building the City

Firstly they wanted to make a name for themselves. They wanted the future generations to know that once upon a time, there were men in the world who had the courage to build a tower, and so they wanted to leave behind them a monument to their pride and ambition. Secondly, the construction of the tower with its top in the heavens was a clear defiance of God, whose word was that they move horizontally and fill the earth. But they refused the horizontal movement in favour of the vertical. Indeed their motive was to compete with God's wisdom. To achieve their goals they needed one leader with building skills. They found such a leader in the person of Nimrod regarding whom we read: 'Cush became the father of Nimrod. He was the first on the earth to be a mighty man. He was a mighty hunter before the Lord, therefore it is said, "Like Nimrod a mighty hunter before the Lord". The beginning of his kingdom was Babel, Erech and Accad, all of them in the land of Shinar' [Gen. 10:8–10].

The ancient and mighty civilizations of Babylon and Assyria are associated with Nimrod. And his character is exactly that of the warrior king of the two civilizations. To Nimrod also is attributed the origin of the military state which extends its empire by sheer and ruthless force. Nimrod is a prototype of the 'Great Man', who by the ruthless and demonic force of his desire for power dominates people and powers. He is said to have been 'mighty before the Lord'! It was God's purpose that made Nimrod mighty – he was the first soldier, the first despotic ruler and the first founder of cities and empires. It is true that the greatness of man is based on God-given qualities. But sometimes leaders use gifts which God has given them as instruments of lust for power and dominion. When a talented leader uses his gifts to obtain absolute powers like Nimrod, the power he obtains corrupts him, and as Lord Acton said, 'Power corrupts and absolute power corrupts absolutely'. The lust for dominion exists at the cost of incalculable suffering and injustice.

There is no doubt that under Nimrod, Babylon and Nineveh became great cities; and according to the biblical story these two cities became synonymous with cruelty, lust, oppression and ruthless power. They stopped acknowledging God as God and became exalted in their pride and in oppression of God's people. Even in New Testament times, Babylon remained a symbol of cruelty, vice and lust for power [Rev. 17:5]. Nimrod aimed at a universal monarchy under the pretence of uniting people 'for their common safety'. His aim was to keep them under one roof so that he could control all of them. But to be a universal monarch is the sole prerogative of God who is Lord of all and King of Kings. Any human being who aims at stepping on to God's throne and bringing the entire human race under his control ends up in failure as the history of the world clearly demonstrates.

Babel Project is Quashed

'And the Lord came down to see the city and the tower which the sons of men had built' [v. 5]; in other words God did not stop the project immediately it was started. He let them continue with their project and God waited patiently until the appropriate time came for him to stop it. This indeed is how God deals with human beings in their reckless quest for towers of Babel. When Russia became a communist state in 1917 and declared itself an atheistic state, God did not intervene immeditely. But during the last few years we have seen the collapse of communism, dramatically demonstrated when the Berlin wall came tumbling down in November 1989. However long the towers seem to last, it is often just a matter of time before they come tumbling down.

God had tried by his commands and admonitions to divert men from this project but all was in vain. And so he took another course to keep the world in some order and tie the hands of those who would not be checked by law.

God said, 'Come let us go down and there confuse their language, that they may not understand one another's language.' This brought the Babel project to a halt, never to be begun again, because the Lord scattered the builders abroad over all the face of the earth. God dealt with the rebels in a most generous and understanding manner. He did not come down in thunder and lightning to consume them. He did not kill them; he only came down, confused their tongues, scattered them and went back.

We note three things. First, their language was confounded and they spoke different languages and could no longer understand one another. Second, this being the case, the project could not continue. The confusion of tongues brought to an end a project which had earlier united the people. The people realized that it was God himself who wanted the project stopped. It is always wise to obey God's voice whenever we realize that it is his will that we stop useless projects. Third, the builders were scattered abroad upon the whole earth [v. 8–9]. They departed in companies, in their families and languages, leaving behind a perpetual memorial of their reproach. The place was called Babel, meaning confusion. Those who are always ambitious to make a great name for themselves often end up miserably.

Lesson for us all

Man seeks by his own virtue and cleverness to build a tower whose top may reach heaven. He seeks to erect a civilization which does not recognize God's grace. But such a civilization is doomed to end in catastrophe and confusion. In the language of the parable, God comes down from heaven in judgement upon secular civilization.

We have, in this country, been building a tower of Babel. At the time of independence we inherited a constitution which allowed more than one party and so we had Kanu, APP and Kadu. But when Kanu won the elections, Kadu and APP dissolved themselves, and this was a great mistake because that is the origin of our present political woes. Attempts by Oginga Odinga to establish another party, Kenya People's Union (KPU) were thwarted. From there we became determined to build the monolithic Kanu party. In June 1982 a Bill was hurriedly passed by parliament to the effect that Kenya became a *de jure* one party state. The idea was that by speaking a 'one party language', Kenyans would be united in accordance to the wishes of 'Nimrod'. The Tower of Babel was even to be symbolized by the actual construction of the (Kanu) Kenya Times Complex at Uhuru Park, whose top would reach the heavens. We give our thanks to this great lady, Professor Wangari Maathai who is with us here today, for bravely fighting single-handedly against the 'Babel project'. God as it were descended and used the voice of Professor Wangari Maathai to confuse the language of the builders and they were scattered.

Kenyans must say 'never again' to towers of Babel. At this particular time in the history of our nation when we are re-establishing a multi-party state, we must be willing to face strong opposition. At the same time we want to discourage the formation of too many parties lest Kenyans become confused. I further strongly suggest that all parties be given equal opportunities both on radio and television and further be allowed to hold public meetings without hindrance. I also warn the new parties to refrain from building towers in the form of a State House and Presidency. And it must be accepted that there is always a winner and a loser; and so the parties that lose must not dissolve themselves.

The story of the Tower of Babel emphasizes that it is man's exaltation of himself over against God which is the prime cause of divisions and rivalries, of which different languages are symbolic. People cannot speak to one another in a common tongue because they have no common interest or mutual regard. God seeks to recreate humanity into one great family, the universal Church, united in the covenant of love in the blood of Jesus Christ, and speaking one common language of the Holy Spirit.

The story of Pentecost with its miraculous reversal of Babel (confusion of tongues) is itself a parable of the power of divine love to bind together men from every nation under heaven in the new covenant of grace [Ac. 2:5–11]. The tongues of fire are actually a Babel story in reverse. When men in their pride boast of achievements, there results nothing but divisions, confusion and incomprehensibility. But when the wonderful works of God are proclaimed, then every person may hear the apostolic gospel in their own tongue. Amen.

19

Stewardship of Creation

Bible Studies delivered during a conference on Environment held at the Sagret Hotel, Nairobi in November 1991, but revised for the purpose of inclusion in this book.

THE SERMON

Introduction

Christianity has often been blamed for the present environmental crises, such as global warming; destruction of forests and expansion of deserts; destruction of species and ecosystems; depletion of non-renewable sources of energy; overpopulation, resulting in food shortage and famine; mismanagement of oceans; and so on.

During a meeting of the American Association for Advanced Sciences held in Washington D.C. on 26th December 1966, Lynn White put forward a thesis that the Judeo-Christian view of the physical creation paved the way for the science and technology that created the environmental crisis. He made the following statements regarding the Christian view of creation:

1. It established a dualism of humanity and nature.
2. It is anthropocentric: nothing in the physical creation has any purpose save to serve the purpose of humanity.
3. Humanity is not part of nature.
4. It insisted that it is God's will that humanity exploits nature for its own ends.

But a careful study of the Bible shows a strong environmental theology.

Creation: The Creator

The whole bedrock of environmental theology is that God is the creator of heaven and earth [Gen. 1:1]. The whole creation is an expression of God and as we begin to understand the creation we also begin to understand something about the creator. Thus Paul says: 'For since the creation of the world God's invisible qualities – his eternal power and divine nature have been clearly seen, being understood from what has been made, so that men are without excuse' [Rom. 1:20].

However, God cannot be identified with his creation because he is distinct from and yet involved in his creation. The Christian concept of creation is: a) theistic. Creation is the work of God. b) *ex nihilo* (Creation from nothing).

The Goodness of Creation

Five times in the first chapter of Genesis we find the refrain, 'And God saw that it was good' [vv. 10, 12, 18, 21, 25]. And in verse 31, after God had created everything, 'he saw all that he had created and it was very good'. This recurrent creation phrase emphasizes the joy and satisfaction of the creator in his work. It also expresses the biblical insight that the world as made by God was in no way defective or marred by evil. This 'good', and 'very good' of God has echoed from the lips of mankind through the centuries in poetry and verse. And so the writer of our conference hymn could say:

> O Lord my God, when I in awesome wonder
> Consider all the works thy hands have made,
> I see the stars, I hear the rolling thunder:
> Thy power throughout the universe displayed.
> Then sings my soul, my saviour God to thee,
> How great thou art! How great thou art!

Just as God saw that all that he had created was very good, we should constantly remind our people to be filled with that awesome wonder as we behold God's creation. When the sun first strikes Mt Kenya early in the morning and from Kabare mission hill in Kirinyaga you can see the mountain valleys, the three famous peaks and the snow, the residents of Kabare should pause and sing 'How Great Thou Art!' Likewise we should be overwhelmed at the sight of Kilimanjaro and Elgon; or when we see the sprawling beauty of the Great Rift Valley escarpment. We should be filled with awesome wonder when we see thousands of colourful flamingos on Lake Nakuru, or when we behold the majestic elephants of Tsavo, the mighty giraffes or the vast assortment of deer on Maasai Mara Game Reserve. The moon and the stars, the singing birds, the crickets, the butterflies; all of these add to the mystifying beauty of creation.

Our worship on Sundays should always include at least ten minutes of celebration of creation. Notice how the Psalmist enjoyed creation:

> O Lord our Lord, how majestic is your name in all the earth! . . . When I consider your heavens, the work of your fingers, the moon and the stars which you have set in place. What is man that you are mindful of him; the son of man that you care for him? [Psalm 8].

The Role of Humanity: Dominion or Domination

On the sixth day God created the living creatures: livestock, creatures that move along the ground – reptiles and the wild animals, man (created in the image of God). The climax of God's activity was the creation of humanity with the mandate to rule over the animals and subdue the earth. The concept of dominion has opened up the accusation that Christian faith is anthropocentric and hence able to dispense with nature as it sees fit.

Dominion: See Genesis 1:28. Two Hebrew words lie at the heart of the matter *Radah* (rule over), and *Kabas* (subdue), a very strong word that could even be translated as 'rape'. Yet, despite the strength of these terms, they do not provide humanity with a mandate to dominate or conquer nature. The meaning of these two words is best seen not in their derivations but in their context, which has two aspects: the cultural mandate and the creation story.

The Cultural Mandate [Gen. 1:26–28]

The cultural mandate is the call for humanity to develop and unfold the creation as the image-bearer of God. Subduing and ruling are one facet of the image of God – hence an essential part of what it means to be human. Subduing and ruling the creation then, are to be done by us as God's representatives. But leadership should be seen as servanthood as exemplified by Jesus himself who emptied himself and became a servant [Phlp. 2].

Creation Story

In the creation story what God created was not merely for humanity. The world and all therein exists for the glory of God. Therefore creation is theocentric and not anthropocentric. The earth is the Lord's not humanity's to do with it as it sees fit. It is God's creation and since we are God's creation and God's delegates we are to take care of it on his behalf. Humanity is accountable to God for its treatment of the earth [Ps. 8:6–9].

The doctrine of *Imago Dei* shows that humanity is created in the image of God and is given responsibility to have dominion over all creation. When the image is obscured, then the dominion is impaired. When the image is restored the dominion is fulfilled. Humankind was created in God's image so that we could co-operate with God in caring for what God has created.

Limits of Dominion

God puts limitations and constrains on dominion. F.W. Welbourn outlines the limitations that God placed on Israel's use of nature: No blood of any animals may be eaten [Lev. 17:10]. Fields are not to be reaped to the border [Lev. 19:9]. Growers may harvest only from trees five years old [Lev. 19:23]. Fruit trees may not be used for siege works [Dt. 20:19]. A kid is not to be boiled in its mother's milk [Dt. 14:21]. An ox is not to be muzzled when treading corn [Dt. 25:4]. A mother bird is not to be taken with its young [Dt. 22:6]. The land is to lie fallow regularly [Lev. 25:1–12]. All the title of the land is the Lord's [Lev. 27:30].

Stewardship of the Earth

Our solidarity with creation should serve to keep us from an oppressive rulership. Dominion is not a dictatorial rulership, i.e. we are not to lord it over creation; rather it is a delegated and accountable rulership. As God's stewards of creation, we will be called upon to account for how we have treated the earth. It should be noted that God did not say that dominion over all creation was reserved only for certain sections of humanity; it belongs to all human beings. Humanity should see itself as God's vicegerent, responsible to God for its stewardship. Otherwise, as Alan Richardson says, 'his science and industry will bring not a blessing but a curse. They will make the earth not a paradise but a dust bowl or Hiroshima' (Richardson A. 'Genesis 1–11:' Torch Bible Paperbacks, 1963, p. 55). Human history is full of sad spectacles of humanity's age long effort to subdue the earth to its own end, and not to God's glory. Proper stewardship of creation brings liberation for nature and humanity because in it we are fulfilling our God-given roles.

Ecological Crisis

The root cause of our ecological crisis is the Fall. In an attempt to become like God, humanity disobeyed God. In Calvin's words, this sin 'perverted the whole order of nature in heaven and earth'. The whole of creation was disrupted. The *Shalom* (peace) that had existed in the garden of Eden between God, humanity and nature was broken. Paul interprets this as a cosmic fall: 'For creation was subjected to frustration not by its own choice but by the will of the one who subjected it, in hope that the creation itself will be liberated from its bondage to decay and brought into the glorious freedom of the children of God' [Rom 8:20–21].

The creation was involved in the consequences of the sin of humanity. 'Cursed be the ground because of you' [Gen. 3:17]. Fallen humanity and its irresponsible exploitation of the earth is the major cause of the ecological crisis. As a result of the fall, the task of fulfilling our cultural mandate becomes all the more difficult. a) Being fruitful, increasing in number and filling the earth became a painful task [Gen. 3:16]. To the woman he said: 'I will greatly increase your pains in child-bearing, with pain you shall give birth to children.' b) Subduing the earth became a painful toil. 'Cursed be the ground because of you, through painful toil you will eat of it all the days of your life. It will produce thorns and thistles for you and you will eat the plants of the fields. By the sweat of your brow you will eat your food until you return to the ground since from it you were taken. For dust you are and to dust you will return' [Gen. 3:17]. c) The struggle with nature is taken up in the following chapters of Genesis. Cain's murder of his younger brother and the cry of Abel's blood to God from the ground has serious consequences. Cain comes under a curse and is driven from the ground and warned that if he tries to till the ground it will not yield crops for him. Hosea takes up the same theme when he writes:

> Hear the word of the Lord you Israelites.
> Because the Lord has a charge to bring
> against you who live in the land.
> There is only cursing, lying and murder,
> stealing and adultery.
> They break all the bounds
> and bloodshed follows bloodshed.
> Because of this the land mourns
> And all who live in it waste away.
> The beasts of the fields and the birds of the air
> and the fish of the sea are dying [Hos. 4:1–3].

Throughout the Old Testament we can see examples of God's concern for the whole of non-human creation. The story of Noah is an example. Noah is commanded to put into the ark every creature according to its kind. So Noah became the first conservationist. Note that the flood was a direct consequence of human rebellion which caused the earth to be corrupt in God's sight. 'Now the earth was corrupt in God's sight and was full of violence' [Gen. 6:4].

The ark and the subsequent covenant that God made with Noah, his descendants and with every living creature is testimony to God's concern for non-human life.

> Then God said to Noah and his sons with him, 'I now establish my covenant with you and with your descendants after you and with every living creature that was with you – the birds, the livestock, and all the wild animals, all those that came out of the ark with you – every living creature on earth. I establish my covenant with you. Never again will all life be cut off by the waters of the flood; never again will there be a flood to destroy the earth' [Gen. 9:8–11]. God's promise that never again shall there be destructive floods illustrates God's concern for the earth.

Calvin B. DeWitt has urged Christians who are committed to an understanding of the scriptures' call to creation to implant three biblical principles for environmental stewardship in their hearts: keeping the creation, giving creation its sabbaths, preserving creation's fruitfulness.

1. The Earth Keeping Principle

Calvin DeWitt reminds us that at the conclusion of many Church services, the blessing should be given which Moses was commanded to tell Aaron and his sons to use in blessing the Israelites: 'The Lord bless you and keep you, The Lord make his face to shine upon you, The Lord be gracious to you and give you peace' [Num. 6:24–26]. The Hebrew word for 'keep' is *Shamar* which means a loving and caring keeping. When we call upon God to bless us and keep us, we are asking God to keep us with all our relationships intact. These include the processes and structures of our own bodies, the interconnections with our community, our connections with the soil, water and air, and our relationships to the sustaining processes of all creation. God's expectation of Adam and Eve was that they would apply this kind of keeping to the garden [Gen. 2:15]. In addition to serving and dressing the garden, they were to keep the garden with all the dynamic relational fullness that this word *shamar* carries. When in accordance with Genesis 2:15 we keep the creation, we make sure that the creatures under our care are maintained with all their proper connections, with members of same species, with the many other species with which they interact, with the soil, and with air and water upon which they depend.

2. The Sabbath Principle

De Witt further reminds us that as we observe the Sabbath of the week to help us to get 'off the treadmill' of continuous work, to help us to 'get things together' again, so too must we give the land its Sabbath rests. The whole purpose of the concept of Sabbath was rest. The seventh day of creation, the Sabbath, was the day when God rested from all the work of creation that he had done [Gen. 2:3]. In the same way the seventh year was to be a Sabbath of rest for the land, and so the Lord said to Moses on Mt Sinai: 'Speak to the Israelites and say to them, "When you enter the land I am going to give you, the land itself must observe a Sabbath to the Lord. For six years sow your fields, and for six years prune your vineyards and gather their crops. But in the seventh year the land is to have a Sabbath of rest, a Sabbath to the Lord. Do not sow your fields or prune your vineyards . . ." ' [Lev. 1–4].

The land and the creatures must be protected from relentless exploitation and must be given what is needed for rejuvenation, as De Witt further says: 'The Sabbath for the land goes beyond agriculture to include all creation – including our use of water and air, discharges into them, our exhausts, smoke, sewage and throwing things away.' We are reminded that failure to give land and creatures their needed rest will result in people no longer being supported by land and creatures. In Leviticus God says: 'But if you do not listen to me and carry out these commands . . ., your strength will be spent in vain because your soil will not yield its crops, nor the trees of the land yield their fruit . . .' [Lev. 26:14, 20].

The people of Israel were warned that if they did not obey God, he himself would scatter them among the nations and he would draw out his sword and pursue them. Consequently, 'Your land will be laid waste, and your cities will lie in ruins. Then the land will enjoy its Sabbath years all the time it lies desolate . . . the land will have the rest it did not have during the sabbaths you lived in it' [Lev. 26:33–35]. God commands us to give creation its Sabbath rests. Just as we need rest, so the soil and the animals also need their Sabbath rest. Every farmer knows that continuous cultivation of the same farm year after year without allowing the land to rest ends by giving diminishing returns.

3. The Fruitfulness Principle

The third principle proposed by De Witt is that we must preserve the fruitfulness of creatures. Before human beings were commanded by God to 'be fruitful and increase in number; fill the earth and subdue it' [Gen. 1:28], God had already given a similar command to the fish and the birds: 'Be fruitful and increase in number, fill the water in the seas and let the birds increase on earth' [Gen. 1:22]. Thus it is God's will that the whole of creation be fruitful, not just people. And thus human fruitfulness must not be at the expense of God's blessing of fruitfulness of other creatures; we violate God's will if our fruitfulness denies blessing to other creatures.

Noah, the first conservationist, understood fruitfulness very well. He obediently brought a sufficient number of each kind of animal into the ark in order to preserve their lives – their genetic continuity. As God provides for creatures, so should we people, who are created to reflect God whose image we bear. We must preserve the integrity of water, land and air; we must preserve the integrity of the biosphere. And with Noah we should preserve the fruitfulness of earth's creatures especially those threatened with extinction, species whose interactions with each other and land and water, form the fabric of the biosphere. Followers of Jesus Christ, imagers of God's love, are preservers of creation's fruitfulness.[1]

1. Quoted from an article 'Take Good Care: it is God's Earth' in *Prism* Dec/Jan 1994 by Calvin de Witt.

The Year of Jubilee [Lev. 25:8–13; Deut. 15]

> Consecrate the 50th year and proclaim liberty throughout the land to all its inhabitants. It shall be a jubilee for you. Each one of you is to return to his family property and each to his own clan.

The Jubilee was the Sabbath year of Sabbath years and meant an extra year of rest for the Jews. Several environmental and ecological considerations underlie the concept of jubilee.

1. It constantly reminded the Jews that the earth was the Lord's. It was not theirs to do whatever they pleased with it. They were stewards and tenants, not owners [Lev. 25:23].
2. It confirms God's care for the land and animals.
3. God demands that we treat his earth and animals with respect; failure to do so by neglecting jubilee and the Sabbath year brought God's judgement [2 Chr. 36:21]. The land enjoyed its Sabbath rests all the time of its desolation. It rested until the seventy years were completed in fulfilment of the words of Jeremiah.

The principle of jubilee demonstrates a distinctively Mosaic understanding of social justice. The jubilee year became the year when the slaves were freed unconditionally and property was returned to bankrupt debtors who had become slaves. Jubilee became an essential sociological model for Israel:

1. The release of enslaved debtors became a metaphor for release of any who were oppressed by injustices.
2. Jubilee became a model for egalitarian people – a sociology which critiqued those structures which kept peace by keeping marginal people marginal and a sociology of equal opportunity which affirmed the endowment of each member of the community with the necessary stamina and talents to achieve and maintain equality with other members of the community.

Jubilee also became an occasion for prophetic critiques of Israel's economy. a) Wealth under jubilary economy was recycled rather than hoarded, redistributed rather than retained, as a way of showing the saving mercies of Yahweh. b) Jubilary economics is rooted in grace not greed. Social structures in keeping with God's grace must advocate a form of justice which shares possessions and redistributes wealth so as to liberate the poor from their material impoverishment.

The principle of jubilee, enshrined in the prophetic word becomes a central feature in the ministry of Jesus. His compassion is directed to the outcasts of this world, his manifesto of mission calls attention to the character of jubilee which is fulfilled in his ministry. Thus when he went to Nazareth on the Sabbath day, he read a passage from Isaiah:

> The Spirit of the Lord is upon me,
> because he has anointed me
> To preach good news to the poor.
> He has sent me to proclaim freedom
> to the prisoners
> And recovery of sight for the blind,
> the release of the oppressed,
> To proclaim the Jubilee year of the Lord's favour [Lk. 4:18–19].

Conclusion: Giving Creation a good Cause for praising the Lord

I cannot find a better way of concluding this essay on environmental theology than to quote Psalm 148 which has been nicknamed 'Choir of Creation'. 'Starting with the angelic host, and celebrating through the skies to the varied forms and creatures of the earth, then summoning the family of man and finally the chosen people, the call to praise unites the whole creation.'[2]

> Praise the Lord from heaven,
> You that live in the heights above.
> Praise him, all his angels, all his heavenly armies.
> Praise him, sun and moon; praise him, shining stars.
> Praise him, highest heavens,
> and the waters above the sky.
> Let them all praise the name of the Lord.
> He commanded and they were created;
> By his command they were fixed in their places forever,
> and they cannot disobey.
> Praise the Lord from the earth,
> sea monsters and all ocean depths;
> lightning and hail, snow and clouds,
> strong winds that obey his command.
> Praise him hills and mountains, fruit trees and forests;
> all animals, tame and wild, reptiles and birds.
> Praise him, kings and all peoples,
> princes and all other rulers; girls and young men,
> Old people and children too.
> Let them all praise the name of the Lord!
> His name is greater than all others;
> His glory is above earth and heaven.
> He made his nation strong,
> so that all his people praise him –
> the people of Israel so dear to him.
> Praise the Lord! [Psalm 148].

2. Kidner, Derek, 'Introduction to Psalm 148' in *Tyndale Old Testament Commentaries, Psalms 72–150* (Inter-Varsity Press, 1975).

20

The Good Shepherd

Ezekiel 34; John 10

Sermon preached at St Andrew's PCEA Church, Nairobi, during a Worship Service, organized by the National Council of Churches of Kenya (NCCK) on Monday, 22nd March 1993, on the eve of the opening of the 7th Parliament. The congregation consisted of newly elected Members of Parliament including the opposition.

THE SERMON

Today is the eve of the seventh parliament which opens tomorrow and I wish to invite you to reflect with me on the biblical metaphor of leaders as shepherds. Jesus said: 'I am the good shepherd' (Jn. 10:12). Any one who has ever looked after animals will agree with me that being a 'shepherd' suggests caring leadership. Every person elected or appointed to the post of leadership: a chief, a district commissioner, a headmaster, a councillor, a member of parliament, the president, a parish priest, a bishop, a moderator; he or she must see himself or herself as a shepherd called to the great task of caring for God's flock.

In John chapter 10 Jesus spoke of the Good Shepherd. In the passage, Jesus outlines a number of qualities of a good shepherd or a good leader.

The first is that he enters the sheep pen by the gate. 'I tell you the truth, the man who does not enter the sheep pen by the gate but climbs in some other way is a thief and a robber.' In other words, any person aspiring to be a leader must not acquire leadership through devious means. It is said that 75% of the members of the sixth parliament actually 'broke' into the chamber. Consequently they could be answerable only to those who had selected them and not to the electorate. It is our belief that the seventh parliament differs from the sixth, in that by far the majority of the elected parliamentarians have entered through the right gate. As for the few who may have broken into the chambers, we pray that they will be found out and dealt with through our esteemed courts. And we sincerely hope and pray that from now on no one will be allowed to get into parliament except through a proper election which is completely free from any form of manipulation. As the majority of this parliament were elected and not selected, we expect vigorous debates; no rubber stamping, and certainly no lack of a quorum.

The second quality of a good leader is that he knows the sheep by name. Jesus said, 'The one who enters by the gate is the shepherd of the sheep. The watchman opens the gate for him and the sheep listen to his voice. He calls his own sheep by name and he leads them out . . . His sheep will follow him because they know his voice' (Jn. 10:3, 4). But they will never follow a stranger, in fact they will run away from him because they do not recognize a stranger's voice. It is, of course, quite difficult for a member of parliament to know all his constituents by name. But even so, the shepherd leader should visit and mingle with the electorate for purposes of familiarization. To this end the Provincial administration should always make it easy for the elected members of parliament from all parties to hold meetings in their constituencies freely and without harassment. This will make it possible for the shepherd leaders to be well informed of the problems affecting their constituents and bring them to parliament.

Third it is the task of the good shepherd to take the sheep to the good pastures. 'I am the gate for the sheep', Jesus said. The gate gives the sheep access to the pastures. Any good and caring shepherd must be greatly concerned about the welfare of the sheep. God, through the prophet Ezekiel, rebuked the leaders of Israel for their sins of commission and omission against the sheep. The shepherds took care only of themselves and neglected the sheep (Ezek.34:2); eating the curds, clothing themselves with wool and slaughtering the choice animals (Ezek. 34:3); neglecting the weak, the sick and the lost, and ruling with harshness (v. 4). As a result of this, the sheep were scattered and wandered all over the mountains and became food for wild animals. My dear councillors and members of parliament, you were elected so that first and foremost you might take care for the flock entrusted to your care. In the past some elected leaders were so skilled in the grabbing of public land that in some of our urban areas there are no plots remaining for such utilities as children's playgrounds, cemeteries, or schools. Poor people have been removed from places where they have lived all their lives, merely to make room for tycoons to put up estates to enrich themselves or to extend their 'vegetable gardens' in the style of King Ahab of old (1 Ki. 21:2).

Concerning the greed and negligence of the leaders of Israel, Ezekiel pronounced this judgement: 'This is what the sovereign Lord says: "I am against the shepherds and I will hold them accountable for my flock. I will remove them from tending the flock so that the shepherds can no longer feed themselves. I will rescue my flock from their mouths, and it will no longer be food for them" ' (Ezek. 34:10). We trust that the new generation of elected leaders will give the highest priority to caring for the poor and the voiceless; in all your efforts to fulfil these tasks, we in the leadership of the Church will give you all possible support, and if you fail to live up to your leadership calling, we shall challenge you fearlessly.

Fourth, the good shepherd protects the sheep from robbers and thieves. 'The thief comes only to steal and kill and to destroy' (Jn. 10:10a). Unlike a hired person who abandons the sheep and runs away when he sees the wolf coming, the good shepherd is willing to lay down his life for the sheep.

Running away from responsibility over the sheep only exposes the sheep to greater danger. The shepherds of Israel regarded their own welfare rather than that of the sheep and so the sheep were plundered and became food for wild animals.

The people of Kenya are looking to the seventh parliament with great expectation, trusting that, by their working together with all other law-enforcing institutions, the politically instigated ethnic clashes in our country, especially in the Rift Valley, Western Kenya and Nyanza Province, will be brought to a quick end. We also expect that the stronger-than-ever voice of parliament, together with the long arm of the law and the government, will bring to an end the banditry in the Eastern and North Eastern provinces and further reduce the rate of violence in our urban centres.

At the present time, the sight of the numerous displaced people in our midst is to be likened to the crowds which Jesus saw, 'harassed and helpless like sheep without a shepherd'. Kenyans should no longer look like this when they have 188 strong shepherds [parliamentarians] to attend to their plight. If these parliamentarians decide to shun their duties, the sovereign Lord says this, 'I will build up the injured and strengthen the weak, but the sleek and strong I will destroy. I will shepherd the flock with justice' (Ezek. 34:16).

And now for the sheep. After challenging the leaders of Israel the Lord had a word for the sheep; he says: 'I will judge between one sheep and another, between rams and goats'. Some of the sheep were trampling on the pasture so that others could not eat. They were drinking water and making the rest of the stream dirty. The strong were butting the weak with their horns. The good shepherd must be ready to step in at any time to stop unnecessary fighting between the sheep. He must stop the strong from exploiting the weak, the poor and the voiceless and further administer justice and bring about reconciliation.

And finally, Jesus the good shepherd says, 'I have come that they may have life and have it to the full', or as another version puts it, 'I have come that they may have life and have it more abundantly' (Jn. 10:10b). Whereas a thief and a robber comes only to steal and to destroy, the good shepherd does exactly the opposite. The purpose of the coming of Jesus Christ is that people might have life and have it more abundantly. At a time when the morale of the people is at its lowest ebb due to the escalating prices of goods, the threat of Aids, unemployment etc., we need to give our lives to the good shepherd, Jesus Christ, who alone can bring new vitality to our nation, and who says, 'I came that they may have life and have it more abundantly.'

Go to parliament and be a good shepherd. In the Name of the Father, Son and the Holy Spirit. Amen.

21

Get Yourself Ready (The Call of the Prophet Jeremiah)

Jeremiah 1:4–19

Sermon preached at the CPK St Peter's Church, Nyeri on 4th July 1993. The occasion was the consecration and enthronement of Rev Alfred Chipman as the first Bishop of the newly created Diocese of Mt Kenya West, and the consecration of the Rev Andrew Adano as the Assistant Bishop of the Diocese of Kirinyaga.

THE SERMON

Jeremiah was born about 640 BC at a place called Anathoth, 3 miles North East of Jerusalem. His call is recorded in the book of Jeremiah 1:4–12. 'Now the word of the Lord came to me saying, "Before I formed you in the womb I knew you and before you were born I consecrated you. I appointed you a prophet to the nations" ' (Jer. 1:4–5).

God had already appointed Jeremiah a prophet even before he was born. But Jeremiah's response revealed a sense of great inadequacy. He started by giving excuses why he could not take up the appointment. 'O Lord God! Behold I do not know how to speak, for I am only a youth' [Jer. 1:6]. The reason for not knowing how to speak was lack of experience. Being only a youth Jeremiah felt he had no experience of speaking. But God could not accept that way of reasoning for he had already chosen and even consecrated him before he was born. Hence the Lord answered Jeremiah: 'Do not say "I am only a youth". For to all to whom I send you, you shall go, and whatever I command you shall speak. Only be not afraid of them, for I am with you and will rescue you, declares the Lord' (Jer. 1:7–8).

Any truly spiritual person called to the ministry of the Church often begins with a feeling of inadequacy and can give all kinds of reasons for feeling unfit for the Lord's service. And this is indeed the major difference between the call to the ministry of the Church and the call to politics. A politician advertizes himself and gives reasons to the electorate why he feels he is the right person to represent them in the County Council or in Parliament. But a person truly called to the ministry of the Church does not go around saying he is the right person to become a pastor or a Bishop. And this is the mistake which Moses made when he felt the call to deliver the children of Israel out of Egypt.

At first he thought he could use his own strength and power without depending on God. When this failed he ran away and was in the university of the desert for 40 years where God prepared him for leadership. And when the day of his calling came, he felt so unfit that he had a long argument with God at the burning bush. Moses, despite his reluctance, was now better equipped for leadership. He was not going to deliver the children of Israel alone – God was going before him to do great things through him. When Peter was called by Jesus to be a fisher of men, he told Jesus, 'Depart from me for I am a sinful man.' But Jesus knew that this man who was so honest that he recognized his sinfulness had the propensity for true discipleship. In a reluctant Peter, Jesus saw a rock on which the Church could be built. It takes a long time for God to recruit people he wants to use to change the world. Those we are going to consecrate bishops today, our dear brothers Alfred Chipman and Andrew Adano, note that God knew you before you were born and he chose you and consecrated you a long time ago. Alfred, do not say 'I am only a *Mzungu* (white man) from Australia.' And you Andrew, do not argue, 'I am only a Gabbra from the Dida Galgalo desert in Marsabit District'. Having been chosen and consecrated by God himself you are from this day destined to be a bishop of the Church.

Remember also that those chosen and prepared by God, emerged at most strategic moments in history. Moses emerged as a leader at the time the children of Israel were crying for deliverance from suffering and slavery in Egypt. Esther became a queen of Persia and Media at a time when there was a plot to kill all the forty thousand Jews who were living in the kingdom. At this crucial time Mordecai her uncle sent a messenger to Esther the Queen so that she in turn could reveal the plot to the king with a hope of stopping the extermination of the Jews. Mordecai told Esther: 'Do not think that because you are in the King's house you alone of all the Jews will escape. For if you remain silent at this time, relief and deliverance for the Jews will arise from another place, but you and your father's family will perish' (Est. 4:14). And then Mordecai tells Queen Esther: 'And who knows but that you have come to your royal position for such a time as this.' In other words, Esther, a Jewess has become the Queen of Persia and Media at a most strategic time in history. Only she must not remain silent.

And who knows but that Alfred Chipman, Andrew Adano, Josiah Were and Horace Etemesi are becoming bishops for such a time as this in the history of Kenya: a time of multi-party democracy, ethnic clashes and economic hardships. Only they must not remain silent. Jeremiah emerged at a time when the nation of Judah was poised on the brink of national and spiritual catastrophe, when the influence of pagan Canaanite worship had exerted a corrupting effect upon Judeans. Religious apostasy had been followed by social and moral decay, and it fell to Jeremiah to present the implications of the Sinai covenant fearlessly in a desperate attempt to stop the destruction of the nation. It is not by accident that this day we should set apart

Alfred Chipman and Andrew Adano as bishops of the Church. God had chosen Jeremiah because he had a special task he wanted him to fulfil. Jeremiah felt inadequate to be a prophet because he thought he was not a good speaker and had no experience. God told Jeremiah, 'You must go to everyone I send you to and say whatever I command you. Do not be afraid of them – Do not fear them.' Fear is the most paralyzing of human emotions. In taking up a position like this, of the first bishop of Mt Kenya West or an Assistant Bishop of Kirinyaga, you may have some fears: fear of possible opposition from some quarters; fear of being misunderstood and misinterpreted; fear of lack of sufficient funds to develop the Diocese; fear of politically motivated thuggery on your house, and so on. No leader is completely free from opposition and the best antidote is courage: God tells Jeremiah, 'Do not be afraid of them, for I am with you to deliver you' (Jer. 1:8).

You will definitely be misunderstood and your sermons will be misquoted. Remember Jesus too was misunderstood and misquoted. The last time I had the privilege of preaching here at St Peter's Church, was in June 1987. During a well-attended civic service, I expounded Daniel 6, the story of how some leaders tried to remove Daniel, a very able civil servant, from his Number Two position in Babylon. At the end of the service the Nyeri District Commissioner, Mr Mwihalule, told me that it was the best sermon he had ever heard. But on the following day he issued a press statement saying that the sermon bordered on sedition. During the whole week I was attacked by politicians who were not present when I preached. They misquoted and misunderstood me. But I was not afraid of them because I was convinced that the truth is, in the final analysis, triumphant. His excellency, the President, brought the debate to an abrupt end by saying, 'Let the Bishop speak.' And so, Alfred and Andrew, go wherever God sends you and say whatever he commands you to tell the people. Remember, ' "They will fight against you, but will not overcome you, for I am with you and will rescue you", says the Lord' (Jer. 1:19). If the Lord is with you to rescue you from them, then there is no cause for fear.

Thus St Paul reminds Timothy: 'Rekindle the gift of God that is within you through the laying on of my hands; for God did not give us the spirit of timidity but a spirit of power and love and self control' (2 Tim. 1:7). Alfred and Andrew, God has called you at this crucial time in the history of this nation so that you may be a prophet, pastor, teacher, preacher, and reconciler, only be not afraid for God promises to be with you.

Jeremiah complained that he did not know how to speak – God had ready treatment for him. He touched his mouth, thus symbolizing the communication of the divine message. God touched his mouth and gave him his letter of reference or job description which we read in verse 10: 'Behold I put my words in your mouth. See I have set you this day over nations and over kingdoms, to uproot and to tear down, to destroy and overthrow, to build and to plant.' Jeremiah's ministry was to nations and kingdoms. It was a national as well as an international ministry. As a result of today's consecrations, you are not just going to be bishops of Mt Kenya West and Kirinyaga. Everywhere you go in Kenya you will be recognized and respected as bishops of the Church. Your ministry should have local, national and international impact. Like Jeremiah, your ministry as bishops of the Church is negative as well as positive. It is negative in the sense that the prophet is called upon to uproot and tear down, to destroy and overthrow. The prophet is commanded to uproot and tear down idols which have been fashioned by human beings. He is called upon to destroy and overthrow the kingdom of Satan. Worship of idols has been defined as, 'worshipping a god that man has created instead of worshipping God who created man'. To worship an idol, in the words of Paul Tillich, is to be 'ultimately concerned with that which is not ultimate'. Objects of idol worship are not bad in themselves until they become objects of worship. Money is a good and indispensable commodity. But money becomes an idol when our minds become focused so much on it, that we go out of our way to exploit others so as to enrich ourselves. We have economic problems today because billions of notes were printed and used to buy votes as well as candidates during last year's elections. Those who defect from one party to another because of money have turned to worshipping money rather than worshipping God. Power can also become an idol. St Paul is right when he says a person who sets his heart on being a bishop, desires a noble task. However, if a person becomes so ambitious to get to the top that he goes about crushing anyone who is an obstacle in his way, then his ambition has become an idol. Instead of concentrating on God so that we may do his will for our lives, we become so power hungry that we end up worshipping an idol of power and not God.

The Christian leader is called upon to destroy and overthrow the kingdom of Satan. The kingdom of Satan is the kingdom of darkness. At this time in the history of our nation we must not underrate the power of Satan. We hear rumours that in our country there are devil worshippers and we doubt the rumour – until a person is arrested here in Nyeri for having killed and eaten a human being and being in possession of witchcraft paraphernalia. Not long ago I intercepted a letter which was purported to have been written from hell by Satan to his followers advising them how to wage war against Christians and the areas they should concentrate on. In times like these, the words of Peter remain relevant to all of us: 'Be self-controlled and alert. Your enemy the devil prowls around like a roaring lion looking for someone to devour. Resist him, stand firm in faith because you know that your brothers and sisters throughout the world are undergoing the same kind of suffering' (1 Pet. 1:8–9). The light of the gospel has come so that the work of darkness can be exposed and the kingdom of Satan defeated.

Positively, the prophet is called upon to build and plant. After plucking and breaking down the idols of our times, and after waging war on the demonic powers of Satan, the prophet must first and foremost build the faith of the flock and plant seeds of righteousness. The bishop is not just a prophet, he is a pastor and a shepherd. He is charged with a responsibility of caring for the Lord's flock, looking for the lost sheep, healing the sick, protecting them from wild animals and from thieves. In his pastoral ministry the bishop will not stay at home waiting for people to come to see him. Rather he will follow the example of Jesus who 'went to every city and village, teaching in their synagogues, preaching the Good News of the kingdom and healing every kind of disease and sickness' (Mt. 9:35). By interacting with the people, Jesus was able to extend his ministry of compassion to them because they were harassed and helpless like sheep without a shepherd. By going out into the towns, villages and manyatta the bishop will be able to see the plight of his people and will find ways and means of 'building' and 'planting'. Bishop Alfred, visit the towns of Karatina, Nyeri, Dol Dol, Othaya, Nanyuki and other towns in your area and see the growing slums, the unemployed youths, and together with other leaders see what may be done. Visit the sick in hospital and see for yourself the victims of Aids; pray for them and give them hope. We have a saying that in every market place there is a mad man. The number of mad people is increasing so much that we should say in every market place there is a mad man and a mad woman. In our ministry, let us try to get to the root cause of the increase in madness. Bishop Alfred should also extend his ministry to the busy businessmen and hard-working market women, to the tea and coffee farmers, to the Maasai cattle herders of Mukogondo, to the civil servants in the Provincial Office here at Nyeri and Nanyuki. As a bishop you are also a pastor to politicians of all parties, to *matatu* drivers and *manambas* (touts), to street children and school children. But you cannot do this work alone. You need the support of a strong team of clergy and laity. Yet, as the overseer, the bishop must go where people are. If you notice any form of harassment and helplessness, do not keep silent. Who knows but that you have become a bishop for such a time as this! May the Lord bless you in your ministry as you seek to uproot and tear down the idols of our time, as you seek to destroy and overthrow the kingdom of Satan and as you build and plant righteousness and truth. As Joshua was commanded: 'Be strong and very courageous, be not frightened, neither be dismayed, for the Lord your God will be with you wherever you go.' In the name of the Father, Son and the Holy Spirit. Amen.

22

Overcoming Satan's Strategies of Ruining the Church

Acts 4–6

Sermon preached on 28th November 1993 on the occasion of fund-raising for St Thomas Cathedral Kerugoya.

THE SERMON

The Book of the Acts of the Apostles was written by Dr Luke, whose main aim was to tell Theophilus the governor about the origins and growth of the Church. The first three chapters portray the tremendous growth of the early Church beginning from the ascension, then Pentecost with its miracles and conversions. We read that on the day of Pentecost, Peter preached so powerfully that 3000 people (men) were added to the Church. This number could have been bigger had they counted women and children. In chapter 3 we find the miracle of the healing of a lame man by Peter and John, as a result of which 2000 more people believed and were added to the Church. There was such a significant growth in the Church that the devil seems to have panicked and so the next three chapters (4, 5 and 6) are all about problems that the Church was encountering. Indeed the three chapters have been described as 'the devil's strategies for spoiling the Church'. We see a three-fold strategy: use of threats, falsehood among members, and, diversion of priorities.

Use of Threats

The most common form of threat that Satan used was persecution. We read that following the miraculous healing of the lame man there was great excitement in Jerusalem. Thousands of people witnessed the miracle and they listened to Peter preaching in the power of the Holy Spirit, and witnessing to the healing power of Jesus Christ.

The government of the day was very worried because Jesus the 'trouble maker' was already dead and buried, and with that they thought the chapter was closed. No wonder they were so shocked to hear that Jesus had risen from the dead. Peter proclaimed: 'The one whom you crucified is the one who has healed this man.' The authorities later summoned Peter and John to appear before the Sanhedrin, the 72-member governing council of Jewish affairs. 'How is it that you healed this man'? they asked the two, who reiterated that it was through the power of the risen Lord. The council strongly warned the two men never to preach in that name again. But Peter and John boldly faced the council and replied: 'You yourselves judge which is right in God's sight, to obey you or to obey God. For we cannot stop speaking of what we ourselves have seen and heard' [Acts 4:19]. Then the council warned them again even more strongly and then set them free. But the apostles went boldly and continued to praise and to speak about Jesus Christ, performing more miracles and wonders through his Name.

The second half of chapter 5 explains how the apostles went on with the healing ministry. In verse 17 we read how the High Priest and all his companions and members of the local party of the Sadducees became extremely jealous of the apostles and hence decided to take action. This time all the apostles were arrested and put into a public jail. We read that in the night an angel of the Lord opened the prison doors and they came out and went to the temple where they began preaching about the New Life. In the morning the Sanhedrin met again and sent for the prisoners but to their great amazement, word came that the prisoners had fled. But the apostles were later found in the temple preaching and they did not resist arrest. Back again before the Sanhedrin, the high priest said to them: 'We gave you strict orders not to preach in the name of this man. But see what you have done, you have spread your teachings all over Jerusalem and you want to make us responsible for his death' [Acts 5:28]. Peter and the other apostles boldly answered back, 'We must obey God, not men. The God of our fathers raised Jesus from death after you had killed him by nailing him to the cross. And God raised him to his right side as Leader and Saviour, to give to the people of Israel the opportunity to repent and have their sins forgiven. We are witnesses to these things, we and the Holy Spirit who is God's gift to those who obey him' (Acts 5:29–32).

When the members of the court heard this they became so furious that they decided to have the apostles put to death. But one Pharisee, whose name was Gamaliel, stood up and said, 'Let the prisoners go out so we can confer.' And after they had gone out, Gamaliel said: 'Men of Israel, be careful what you are about to do with these men because there was a time when there was a man called Thaddeus claiming to be somebody and about 400 people followed him. But he was killed and all his followers scattered and his movement died down. The same with Judas the Galilean; he too had a big following but when he was killed his people were scattered. And so in this case I tell you, do not take any action against these men. Leave these people alone for if this plan and work of theirs is a man-made thing, it will disappear but if it comes from God, you cannot possibly defeat them and you could find yourselves fighting against God' (Acts 5:35–39).

The words of Gamaliel must have convinced the council in a great way and so they called in the apostles again. They were whipped and given a further warning not to preach in that name, and then set free. The apostles left the court joyfully, thanking God that they were considered worthy to suffer disgrace for the name of Jesus. Every day in the temple and in people's homes they continued to teach the Good News about Jesus the Messiah.

Therefore Satan's first strategy of using threats against the believers failed. It is a fact even today, that the voice of the Church can never be strangled! Hence it is useless for any government to try and silence the Church. When Russia became a communist country, the government tried to deny the existence of God and so they persecuted the Church severely and many Churches were closed down. It almost appeared that Christianity in Russia had died. But the Church only went underground and as soon as communism was dismantled in 1989, the Church of Christ came back to life. The Church in Russia is now among the fastest growing Churches in the world.

One of the most difficult periods of my ministry as bishop was 1988 and '89 when we publicly started to challenge the evils of election-rigging. I was threatened from all sides and many of you witnessed some of these threats in this very Church when a scoundrel known as Waguthira came forward, wanting to snatch the microphone from me. Shortly after this incident, they harassed me outside our diocesan bookshop here in Kerugoya town. Things did not end there and you know very well that on the night of 22/23rd April 1989, only two weeks later, they came to my home at night, shouting that they had been sent to kill me. They raided my house and did a lot of damage. The story is well known of how I climbed onto the roof of the house, from where I shouted for help and when neighbours came, the raiders panicked and ran away in great disarray. Shortly after the raid on my house, a big meeting attended by all the leaders from Central Province was held here at Kerugoya and the sole agenda of the meeting was to issue threats and abuses to me and to frighten me to *nyamaza* (keep quiet). But the more they threatened us, the more we spoke out boldly. If I may ask, where are all those people now? *Warugaga, niatobokaga, Wainaga nieroragira, Mucera na mukundu akundukaga o take* (he who used to jump across a stream now plunges in, he who used to dance, now merely spectates, and, bad company ruins good morals).

I would like to advise the current government to leave the Catholic bishops alone; their pastoral letter for which they are being harassed was excellent. And for the government to keep referring to that letter as though it were a very bad one is wrong. If they were wise they could just have read the letter and noted it. For the more they talk about it with such bitterness the more they encourage the public to want to read it; and of course those who read it will agree with it. When the bishops talk about violence in this country, when they speak about the clashes in the Rift Valley, they do so because they are convinced that God wants them to speak. And so whenever the government orders us to keep quiet we shall ask them, 'Are we going to obey you or God?' On our part we have chosen to obey God and not men. Nothing could deter the apostles from proclaiming the gospel, not even arrest. We shall overcome Satan's strategy by being bold!

Unity of Believers and subsequent Falsehood

'The group of believers was one in mind and heart. No one said that any of his belongings was his own, but they all shared with one another everything they had. With great power the apostles gave witness to the resurrection of the Lord Jesus and God poured rich blessings on them all. There was no one in the group who was in need . . . . And so it was that Joseph, a Levite born in

Cyprus and whom the apostles called Barnabas, (which means "one who encourages"), sold a field he owned and brought the money to the Apostles' (Acts 4:32–34).

The spirit of fellowship was tremendous – those who were rich voluntarily sold what they had and brought the proceeds to the apostles for distribution, and the best example in this kind of giving was Barnabas. But some other members of the Church were the complete opposite of Barnabas. Ananias and his wife Sapphira had made a similar pledge that they would sell part of their property and bring everything to the apostles for distribution. Now, what Barnabas and this couple did was more or less the same because both had sold land. But the difference was that Barnabas brought everything as he had promised, but Ananias and Sapphira did not honour their pledge, they took half the money, pretending that that was all, and pocketed the rest. But if only they had pledged to pay half of the proceedings, that would have been fine, and so their sin was falsehood, a strategy of the devil. From the moment they had committed their proceeds to God they could not use it as they pleased, for that would be embezzlement of God's funds. Hoping to be congratulated by Peter, Ananias came and presented his donation. Then Peter said to him: 'Ananias, why did you let Satan take control of you and make you lie to the Holy Spirit by keeping part of the money you received for the property? Before you sold the property it belonged to you; and after you sold it, the money was yours. Why then did you decide to do such a thing? You have not lied to men, you have lied to God!' [Acts 5:3–4]. And as soon as Ananias heard that, he developed a heart attack and died instantly. Of course there were no telephones those days to telephone Sapphira and inform her of her husband's death. And so about three hours later Sapphira came in confidently, hoping to be congratulated by Peter. She must have shuddered within when Peter asked her directly: 'Tell me, was this the full amount you and your husband received for your property?' And with every bit of courage left, Sapphira brought herself to say, 'Yes'. Peter could stand it no more and he angrily said to her, 'Why did you and your husband decide to put the Holy Spirit to test? The men who buried your husband are at the door right now and they will carry you out too. At once she fell down at his feet and died . . .' [Acts 5:1–11].

The devil wanted to interfere with the life of the Church by perpetuating falsehood among believers. The first lesson we learn from this is that hypocrisy is a sin against the Holy Spirit. Again, falsehood ruins fellowship. If the hypocrisy of Ananias and Sapphira had not been exposed, it would have ruined the fellowship of the young Church. The third lesson we learn is the importance of discipline in the Church for purposes of safeguarding its dignity.

Diversion of Priorities

In chapter 6 we read that as the number of disciples kept growing, there developed a quarrel between the Greek speaking Jews and the native Jews. The Greek speaking Jews said that their widows were being neglected in the daily distribution of funds. So the twelve apostles called the whole group of disciples together and said, 'It is not right for us to neglect the preaching of God's Word in order to handle finances.' So the apostles appointed the seven deacons to carry out the distribution of funds and food.

It appears that the Church was experiencing tremendous growth and many people were bringing money from the sale of property. This must have overwhelmed the apostles and they became completely involved in the distribution of money and food to the widows. And then complaints started coming, that there was unfairness in the distribution. When these complaints came the apostles did not just sweep the matter under the carpet. Instead they called the people together, discussed the matter and the apostles realized they had been wrong in their priorities. They had been appointed first and foremost to preach the good news of Jesus Christ; other people could carry out the administration.

Those of us who have been called to minister the word of God must take the same view of our priorities. You cannot be the vicar and at the same time the treasurer, and so on. You cannot do everything. There are other people greatly talented in those areas who would be very willing to be of assistance. We need to mobilize everybody in the Church to make his or her contribution.

It is my personal feeling that as a bishop of the Church I do not need to stand for parliamentary elections because my first priority is to preach the Good News of Jesus Christ. If a time comes when I feel I want to go there, I shall first resign or retire and then go into parliament. Yet I am convinced that we can speak more powerfully from the pulpit and change the course of the history of our nation. Indeed we have achieved more through the pulpit than those who go to the august house. We must not allow the devil to win the battle against the Church. We must never allow him to scare us. We must declare the whole counsel of God to the people of this nation and caution those involved in corrupt ways and who are bent on making gains at the expense of the poor. Barnabas was greatly concerned about the plight of the poor. That's what a good leader should be like. Our leaders should be thinking more about the poor and those who have nowhere to call home. Unfortunately this is not the case. Let me ask: Why do people who already have acres and acres of land want to grab even more when we have so many landless families around us? Very rich individuals have been buying off the Trust land that some of these families have been depending on. I am surprised that if a rich person wants land, he gets free land so easily, but that's not the case with the poor people.

Right opposite this Church, on the other side of the road, there is a plot of land which belongs to Kerugoya hospital. It is Plot No. 235 and, as far as I can remember, the first house ever built for a doctor in Kerugoya was built there. And the first doctor ever to treat me was living there, Dr Angawa. Now on that plot, there is a government house but the plot has already been given to an individual who has now subdivided it into plots 235 and 275. The developer of No. 275 has already gathered building materials and is preparing to put up a multi-storey complex for his own personal benefit. I would like to ask the county council or the municipality to rectify that situation. I protest in the strongest terms possible against the grabbing of that hospital plot. It is very immoral for an individual to grab public land for his own personal use. And so I say, 'Return plot 235 and 275, whoever you are!' May God help us as we strive to stand against the work of the devil and as we boldly proclaim the whole counsel of God. In the Name of the Father, Son and the Holy Spirit. Amen.

23

Called to be Peacemakers

Sermon preached on 5th December 1993 during the consecration of the Rt Rev Julius Gatambo as the 2nd Bishop of the Diocese of Mt Kenya Central. The service was held at the St James and All Martyrs' Cathedral Church, Murang'a.

THE SERMON

It is most likely that the sermon on the mount was preached immediately after Jesus chose the twelve disciples. It has therefore been called 'the compendium of Christ's doctrine', 'the *magna carta* of the Kingdom' and 'the manifesto of the King'. In this sermon we have the core and the essence of the teaching of Jesus to the inner circle of his chosen men.

The very fact that Jesus sat down to teach his disciples is an indication that the teaching is central, official, authoritative, and the very essence of his teaching. Julius Gatambo, we are about to consecrate you and enthrone you as the Bishop of Mt Kenya Central; let this throne not be just a decoration for St James & all Martyrs' Cathedral. From time to time, speak ex-cathedra when the spirit urges you to prophesy.

Peace

Our deepest desire as human beings is peace; peace in our hearts, with our neighbours, in our nation, with the environment, peace in the world. Any one who helps to bring about peace becomes a peacemaker. And blessed are the peacemakers for they shall be called sons of God. Jesus did not talk about peace lovers. It is quite possible for someone to be a peaceful person while he is very far from becoming a peacemaker. A person may know that there is something wrong in a given situation; in the village, at school, at Church or in society. But that person may feel that to involve himself in trying to rectify the situation will land him in unnecessary trouble. Hence he will say; 'For the sake of peace, I will keep away'. But his failure to intervene worsens the situation. By keeping a safe distance that person becomes a peace lover. You must have come across a big crowd watching two people fighting and none among the spectators has the courage to intervene, arguing that if you dare to intervene, you could end up getting beaten up yourself. Therefore for the sake of peace someone feels he would rather remain a spectator. But a peacemaker would move forward and try to stop the fighting even if there were risks involved. In essence a peace lover is a trouble maker, for the longer a dangerous situation is allowed to continue, the more serious the consequences and the harder it becomes to resolve them.

Students of history know very well that the Second World War could have been avoided had the great powers of Britain, France, and USA taken a more vigorous and tough policy against Hitler. Instead they adopted the policy of appeasement. In order to avoid war they allowed Hitler to take Austria and Czechoslovakia. International diplomacy reached its lowest ebb when Neville Chamberlain, the Prime Minister of Britain, returned from Munich saying he had brought peace with honour, after allowing Hitler to take Austria. Before very long that very gesture of appeasement led inevitably to the Second World War, during which at least six million Jews and thousands of other people are believed to have been slaughtered, and the world was put into total chaos. The saying, 'If you want peace, prepare for war', may have its relevance in the world of politics and international diplomatic relations. It, however, has no theological validity. The best theology can offer are those words of Jesus, 'Blessed are the peacemakers . . .' Julius Gatambo, may I dare to indicate that you are becoming bishop at a time when Kenya desperately needs peacemakers. That is the biggest challenge to your ministry as a bishop. But what are the qualities of a peacemaker?

1. He must hunger and thirst for righteousness.

Think of the kind of hunger that grips a person in a situation of famine in which he may go for many days without having anything to eat. And the thirst that Jesus talks about is the kind experienced by a desert dweller, who, unless he drinks water, will surely die. To be a peacemaker we must hunger and thirst for righteousness as a starving person hungers for food and as a desperately thirsty person longs for water. A peacemaker must have a hunger and thirst for goodness which is total and complete.

2. A peacemaker must be courageous.

A peacemaker who is a coward is a contradiction in terms. St. Paul told the young Timothy, 'For this reason I remind you to keep alive the gift that God gave to you when I laid my hands on you. For the spirit that God gave us does not make us timid; instead his spirit fills us with power, love, and self control (2 Tim. 1:6–7). And when Joshua was being commissioned to lead Israel in place of Moses, God told him, 'Be strong and very courageous. Do not be terrified, do not be discouraged. For the Lord your God will be with you wherever you go' [Josh. 1:7–9].

These are not days for cowardly bishops. A bishop must be strong and courageous and must not be terrified by threats from any quarters. As one writer has said, 'The one thing one should fear most is fear itself.' A peacemaker must therefore be prepared to go where there is trouble. You cannot be a peacemaker and at the same time refuse to get involved in situations where a peacemaking process is needed. Politicians are to be commended for choosing a career that is full of ups and downs and which is beset by troubles. But the call to politics is a call to a career of peacemaking.

The original meaning of 'politics' in the Greek world was 'the welfare of the *Polis*' or the city. Those involved in politics must seek the welfare of the nation and must actively work for peace.

Our quarrel with politicians is when they tell Church leaders to keep silent about politics and concentrate on spiritual matters. They want to be the sole peacemakers and they would prefer that bishops stay passively as peace lovers. That cannot be! The bible teaches us that a human being is a psychosomatic unit, a unity of *psyche* and *soma* (i.e spirit and body) and the two cannot be separated.

When we are hungering and thirsting for justice, the spirit urges us to challenge injustices in our nation – rigging of elections, corruption in high places, political assassinations, politically motivated clashes etc. As peacemakers, bishops and pastors have to be involved in the quest for justice; after all politics is so important that it cannot be left to politicians alone. Left on their own they have created the 'Hiroshimas' of their world, which in our nation at this present time include West Pokot, Molo, Enoosupukia, Burnt Forest etc, where clashes have continued unabated. (And now we hear there are marauding youths in Kwale district of Coastal Province). A bishop should never listen to those who tell him to keep quiet when the people are bleeding; we cannot keep quiet when Cain has struck once more while asking, 'Am I my brother's keeper?'

3. A peacemaker must be a man or woman of Faith.

Because of this overwhelming faith in God, the peacemaker believes that in the final analysis truth will always be triumphant and peace will be achieved. We can draw a great lesson on faith from the story of Blondin, the great French gymnast who not only walked across the mighty Niagara Falls on a rope; he also walked with a loaded wheelbarrow. We hear that when he asked a small boy to get into the wheelbarrow for a ride across the Falls the boy ran away as fast as his feet could take him. In other words he believed that Blondin could do wonders but he did not want to commit himself. He believed, but he did not have faith.

The writer of the letter to the Hebrews has defined faith as 'the assurance of things hoped for, the conviction of things not seen' (Heb. 11:1). We might also describe faith as the willingness with which we place ourselves in the wheelbarrow of Jesus so that he can take us across the 'Niagara Falls' of this world. Hence we sing in Kikuyu: '*Wihoke Mwathani rugendoini*' (Trust the Lord all the way. . .)

4. Peacemakers must be prepared to take risks.

Risk and faith go together. If you are not prepared to take a risk then you have no faith. The process of peacemaking can be very risky, but unless we are prepared to get involved in the process irrespective of the risks, we cannot achieve much. However, we must be wise in taking risks. I remember one lady theologian in a conference saying, 'God does not only want his messengers to die for the gospel; he would also want them to live for the gospel.' Thus Jesus told his disciples that when the awful horror comes, 'those who are in Judea must run to the hills'. A peacemaker must not allow himself to be killed for no good cause. And so, 'if they come through the door, escape through the window, and if they come through the window, go to the rooftop and hide there.' (At this juncture there was a lot of laughter and applause as the congregation recalled the 1989 raid on the Bishop's house, during which he ran to the rooftop from where he called for help).

5. A peacemaker must be a reconciler.

The work of a reconciler is to bring together people who have been enemies. The reconciler does not take sides until he has fully established the truth of the matter. Only then can he take the side of the truth. The reconciler should be able to show those who are wrong where they have gone wrong and then patiently work hard to effect reconciliation.

6. A peacemaker must be incorruptible.

Corruption is a major cause of instability in Kenya today. You and I are poorer now due to various financial scandals in high places. Poverty causes instability. Peacemakers themselves must neither give nor accept bribes. They must not allow themselves to be silenced by any offer of *Sima* or *Pilau* or money. The peacemakers must be consistent in their crusade to bring about peace.

7. The peacemaker must be at peace with himself, his neighbour and with God.

There are two types of people in this world. There are those who are storm centres of trouble and bitterness and strife. Wherever they are, they are either involved in quarrels themselves or are cause of quarrels between other people. They can even use remote control methods to encourage other people to cause problems in the Church or in society. These people are trouble-makers. There are people like that in every society, and such people are doing the devil's work. But thank God that there are also people in whose presence bitterness cannot live; people who bridge the gulfs, who heal breaches and who sweeten the bitterness. Such people are doing a God-like work, for it is the great purpose of God to bring peace between men and women and himself and between persons. Blessed are peacemakers for they do God-like work and may therefore be called sons of God! Shalom.

24

Let the Farmer Have the First Share of His Labour

Sermon preached at Wang'uru, Mwea on 16th January 1994 during a Service of Thanksgiving for the people of Mwea Archdeaconry in Kirinyaga District.

THE SETTING

On 21st December 1993 the Rural Dean of Kutus deanery wrote to inform me that 60 acres of public land commonly known as Red Soil on the Kimbimbi – Ngurubani road had been grabbed by a few powerful people, and that the district surveyor had been ordered to subdivide the land into 3 or 2 acre plots. A land agent based at Kerugoya was selling the plots on behalf of the grabbers at Ksh 60,000 per acre. Soon after Christmas I visited the Red Soil area and found the surveyors very busy subdividing the land and marking the boundaries.

The Mwea rice is grown on the black cotton soil but in various parts of the Mwea irrigation scheme there are many patches of red soil which were given to rice farmers for free use so that they could grow alternative crops for the purpose of a balanced diet.

About 36 years ago an ex-Mau Mau detainee by the name of Njoroge Njire was given a four-acre rice farm at Mathangauta, and was also allowed to grow vegetables on a two-acre red soil plot. When he migrated to Nakuru, his son, Jeremiah Kamau, inherited both the rice farm and the two-acre red soil plot. He and his wife Keziah have five sons and a daughter. For many years they have been growing horticultural crops on the two-acre plot, but towards the end of 1993, the plot was sold by a new 'owner' to Mr Kinyua from Kiangwenyi village near Mt Kenya forest, for about Ksh.120,000. This meant that Jeremiah and his wife Keziah who had cultivated the land for over 30 years were going to be evicted from the plot.

This is what provoked me to organize a special Service in Mwea on 16th January 1994. The Service which was held at the Wang'uru Secondary School was attended by thousands of people from Mwea and other parts of Kirinyaga District. In my sermon I dwelt on two major issues of great concern: landlessness (and land grabbing), and exploitation of the Mwea farmer.

THE SERMON

In Paul's second letter to Timothy chapter 2:4–6, we read: 'A soldier on active duty wants to please his commanding officer and so does not get mixed up in the affairs of civilian life. An athlete who runs in a race, cannot win the prize unless he obeys the rules. The farmer who has done the hard work should have the first share of the harvest.'

We have gathered here this morning to give thanks to God for the great things he has done for us. Indeed, it is the duty of Christians to live lives of thanksgiving to God for all his goodness. But in addition to giving thanks, we must also search our hearts and seek to put right things that are not right in our lives and in our society. So in my sermon this morning, I have two special issues to address: 1. The hard working Mwea Farmer; 2. The issue of landlessness in Kirinyaga District.

The Hard-Working Farmer

Paul tells Timothy that the hard-working farmer should be the first to receive the share of the crops [v. 6]. St Paul was very fond of using imagery to facilitate quick comprehension. In this particular case, he draws in our minds the picture of a soldier, an athlete, and a farmer. A Christian is likened to a soldier, an athlete, and a farmer.

A Christian as a soldier

A soldier is a very disciplined person. If there is war he gives first priority to going on the battlefield where he obeys the instructions of the commanding officer without question. At such a time he must not get entangled with the affairs of civilian life for his first priority must be the defence of his country. A Christian is like a soldier who must first and foremost be on the battlefield, following the instructions of this commanding officer, Jesus Christ who must be obeyed without question.

A Christian as an athlete

For an athlete to win a race, he has to do a lot of regular practice; running every morning and evening. And during the competition he has to observe the rules of the contest.

A Christian as a farmer

Paul likens a Christian to a hard-working farmer. He says the hard-working farmer should be the first to receive the share of his crop. A good farmer cultivates his land at the right time, he plants the seeds at the right time, he weeds at the right time and then he waits patiently until the time when the harvest comes and it is such a farmer whom Paul says should have the right of his crop.

The Mwea Farmer

1. The Horticultural Farmer.

Although Mwea is predominantly a rice growing region, we know that over a number of years an agricultural revolution has taken place here in Mwea and the people have shown a real determination to turn an area formerly known for its dryness and unproductivity to a haven of horticultural production. And so, amidst other things, by use of furrow irrigation, Mwea has suddenly become the biggest producer of horticultural products in Kenya. Most of the French beans that are exported outside the country are grown in Mwea. 'Where there is a will there is a way', goes the saying, and this has been very true for the people of Mwea.

My concern is that the farmer who is working so hard should be the first to get the main profits of his crop. I am sure there are many people here who are growing French beans. Last night I telephoned someone in England who imports the French beans (otherwise known as Kenya beans) and he says that Kenya has had a monopoly in the production of French beans over any other country in Africa but that of late Zimbabwe has entered the race and is competing with Kenya considerably in the export of the beans. From the telephone conversation I gathered that the broker gets over 300% profit! But, if I may ask, who is worthy of greater benefit from the sale of French beans? The broker or the farmer? Yet we see that it is the exporter who is benefiting from the crop. The buyer in England, to whom I talked last night, asked me to advise the farmers of *Miciri* (French beans) to form a co-operative. Otherwise they will only continue to be exploited by the middlemen. Paul says that it is the hard-working farmer who should be the first to receive the share of his hard work. And you will all agree that growing *miciri* is not like growing maize; it involves a lot of careful attention and much work for 45 full days when you start harvesting the crop. Yet the person who takes the greatest profit from your hard labour is a middleman who played no part at all in the production. Therefore, I urge you again and again, you my brothers and sisters who are growing *miciri* to think seriously about forming a co-operative.

Just the other day President Moi himself acknowledged that in Kirinyaga we are growing more French beans than anywhere else in Kenya, and if that's the case, Mwea must be leading the production. It is also known that most of the tomatoes that are consumed in Nairobi actually come from Kirinyaga, and once again Mwea must be leading.

God has given us a wonderful country (Kirinyaga) which does not lack water, land or food and as long as we are able to use our brains productively, this will always be the case; more so now that land seems to be getting scarce because of the growing population.

The Exploited Rice Grower

The major occupation of the people of Mwea is the growing of rice. For many years the sprawling plains of Mwea had been left as a Reserve. Animals wandered over it and the land used to be cared for by our forefathers until a time came when the Mwea Irrigation Scheme was formed around the time of the Mau Mau Emergency and rice growing was started. The first tenants at the Mwea irrigation scheme were the Mau Mau ex-detainees. This became one of the most successful projects in the world and indeed there is nowhere else in Kenya where so much rice is grown. Actually 75% of all rice grown in Kenya comes from Mwea; and note that Mwea rice is more delicious than any of the other imported brands of rice.

I believe that credit should be given where credit is due and that where things have gone wrong they should be corrected. And I say these things in good faith so that they can be rectified for the good of the people of Mwea. One of our prime concerns is the health of the people who grow rice because there was a time when bilharzia was very common among the farmers. We are grateful that a research station on bilharzia has been set up. But we know the disease is still very far from being eradicated and for this reason we are asking the government to speed up the mechanisms involved in order to save the health of thousands who are working so hard to produce rice for the nation. In places like Japan, where they grow rice, the government dealt with the disease and almost eradicated it.

There is also an allegation that some years back the rice farmers lost 80 million shillings through a tax error by the National Irrigation Board (NIB). There is also an allegation that 50 million was put into a 'political' bank, which later became bankrupt and so the 50 million shillings disappeared into a bottomless pit.

The other allegation has to do with the rice bonus for farmers. In 1985, His Excellency the President ordered that rice farmers be paid a bonus and for the next three years the farmers were paid. But since that time no bonus has been paid except that 1.2 million shillings was paid recently but that was actually arrears for 1988. For six years now the farmers have not been paid any bonus, and so the NIB owes rice farmers over 7.2 million shillings in bonus. The NIB should come out openly and tell us where the farmers' bonus has gone. We want to reiterate Paul's words that the farmer should be allowed to benefit from his hard labour. This bonus should be paid to the farmers as they are the most deserving.

Rice milling charges:

There was a time when the rice milling charge per kilogramme was Ksh 2.50 which was quite a benefit to the farmers who are share holders as the mill was making a lot of money. So when the charge was reduced to 86 cents per kilo, the farmers lost in dividends. We strongly suggest that these complaints be studied with a view to correcting them and to ensure that the tenants who are working so hard get the right returns for their hard labour.

Annual General Meeting:

Any Co-operative society worth its name always holds an annual general meeting for its members. This should be not only a common but also a mandatory practice and rice farmers have the right to demand for an AGM to be called since they are all share-holders of their society. They need to be presented with the audited accounts every year, in addition to other reports concerning their farming, and further be allowed to ask questions. But surprisingly, for the last 26 years, there has never been an Annual General Meeting. We are therefore emphatic in our request that AGMs be effected forthwith.

Broken Rice:

This is the rice that separates from the good rice during milling and it rightfully belongs to Mwea Rice Mills & Co. as per Government Act Chapter

4.86. The National Irrigation Board (NIB) gets 55% and the shareholders 45%. The 45% share of broken rice should automatically be made available to the farmers at all times. But in September 1993, there were many complaints and questions as to where the 45% goes because farmers were not getting it. We have found out that some of our own leaders are involved in the corruption and are making very quick money while the local business women queue for hours, and all they get is the worst grade, the broken of the broken. I am told that these big people buy the broken rice at Ksh500 per bag and sell it at Ksh1,400 thus making a profit of Ksh900 per bag, without any hard work. The rice farmer spends so much time and energy cultivating rice and others shamelessly harvest where they have not planted. This is exploitation of a serious kind especially when it is done by people who are our leaders and who are therefore supposed to be minding our welfare. Ezekiel says, 'You are doomed you Shepherds of Israel.' The leaders of Israel were severely reprimanded for neglecting the welfare of the people and thinking only about themselves.

> You take care of yourselves but not the sheep. You drink their milk, wear clothes made from the wool and kill and eat the finest sheep. You have not taken care of the weak ones: you have not healed those that are sick; you have not bandaged those that are hurt; you have not brought back those that wander off; you have not looked for those that are lost. Instead you have treated them cruelly (Ezek. 34: 2–4).

I would say to those who have been exploiting rice farmers, wherever they are, whether they are in administrative offices, whether they are in positions of power, in the name of God, let them stop it!

The Rich Asians:

We hear that the 55% share of the broken rice which goes to the National Irrigation Board is usually sold to rich Asians in Nairobi. Hence the Asians also are gaining from your hard work. It would be better if the 55% is sold directly to the farmers so that they receive the greater benefit.

But I would also like to challenge the people of Mwea not to remain silent until the Bishop speaks. Speak, whenever you see things going wrong. Know your rights and defend them without fear.

Landlessness in Kirinyaga

We are greatly concerned about the people who are landless in this district. At Kiorugari, there are 88 landless families. At Kangaita there are 16 roadside families. At Githogondo there are 300 and at Kimomori there are very many people who are cultivating there and who are now being asked to leave so that the land can be divided by the clan. There are also many people who are living at Mwambao near Rupingazi who have no proper farming land, and I know there are many, many other people who are landless in this district. My concern is that leaders in this district seem to be thinking more about people who have got land and not about those who are landless. If there is any land anywhere that needs to be given out, why can't they consider the very desperate cases of landless people in the district? Certain red soil portions in Mwea were deliberately set aside by the NIB so that the tenants can have a place to grow supplementary crops like maize, beans and varieties of horticultural crops. Some of this red soil land was supposed to be used for the compensation of more than 100 farmers from Kandongu whose land was compulsorily taken for the expansion of the rice scheme. But I was surprised that even the District Commissioner of Kirinyaga at that time, Mr Joseph Mengich, and the man in charge of special branch, Mr Seurey, were given ten acres each when they least deserved it. Immediately they received the land, they sold it and pocketed the money.

That was three years ago. Now I hear that the 60 acres of the red soil land that is used by Mathangauta and Murubara rice farmers is also up for grabs. Someone has ordered that the land be sub-divided into portions of 3 acres each and the district surveyor team spend most of their time there subdividing that land. The district surveyor was still there yesterday and the day before with a land-rover, registration No. G.K. SS075. They are sub-dividing that land. We do not know who has given them the authority to sub-divide it. An agent has been entrusted to do the rest of the survey work, ensuring that people pay the money and get the title deeds straight away. An acre is being sold for 60 (or 70) thousand shillings.

The big question is, if this land has to be subdivided, why can't they divide it among the tenants who have been cultivating it all this time? Once it has been sold out to strangers, what is going to be the plight of these tenants? The other question is, who is getting the Ksh60,000 from each acre? If the land is 60 acres, that in effect is 3 million shillings. Yet the money from this public land is not being paid to the government; rather it is going into the pockets of a few influential leaders, including civil servants. We want to challenge those involved in the selling business to tell us where they are taking the money. Even if it is the District Commissioner, let him tell us where he is taking the money and why land is being sold to the rich people when there are so many landless people in Kirinyaga District. What considerations are we giving to the landless people? Note that once that land has been divided, it is going to be fenced and if you dare to walk there you could easily be charged with trespassing.

This kind of situation cannot work for peace and prosperity in Kirinyaga District. The people of Kiorugari come to my office nearly every week wanting to know about the 50 acres near Kimbimbi which were fenced off by a very rich person who warned them not to dare to walk there any more. These people have got children whom they would like to feed and to take to school. That farm used to help them greatly. 'Love your neighbour as yourself', the Bible says. But is this the way you love, people of Kirinyaga? I would also like to let you know that here in Ngurubani there is nowhere to construct a sewage works, there is nowhere to build a cemetery, there is nowhere to build a hospital. And the same can be said of Kutus and Kerugoya. We should really consider how we are going to re-plan Kirinyaga District; plans that are carefully drawn up, so that we can leave space for our children to play, for hospitals to be built and so on. What seems to be happening now is what Micah the prophet warned about when he said:

> How terrible it will be for those who lie awake and plan evil! When morning comes as soon as they have a chance, they do the evil they planned. When they want fields they seize them. When they want houses they take them.

As the Lord says, 'I am planning disaster on you and you will not escape it. You are going to find yourself in trouble, and then you will not walk proudly anymore' (Mic. 2:1).

Micah further gives hope to those who are oppressed: 'But I will gather you together, all you people of Israel that are left. I will bring you together like sheep returning to the fold. Like a pasture full of sheep, your land will once again be filled with many people' (Mic. 2:12).

There is always hope for God's people. God always intervenes at our point of greatest need. It is our prayer that the land we are talking about (between Mathangauta and Murubara) will not be taken away. The people who are surveying, please stop surveying that land! And you prospective buyers, stop paying that money! And to you who have been working that land all these years, I say, speak out and do not wait until the Bishop speaks. They have been saying that the Bishop has kept quiet for too long. I am not quiet. Follow us and hear what we are saying. And we shall continue to talk and to point out injustices in our midst. May God's people be protected from exploitation. May the farmer get the share of his hard work and may God bless you the people of Mwea and Kirinyaga.

THE AFTERMATH OF THE SERMON

The following Monday after the service, the 'Nation' and 'Standard' newspapers published part of the sermon, especially where I had said that the red soil land had been grabbed by some civil servants. The following day the Kirinyaga District Commissioner, Mr Francis Sigei, issued a press statement, challenging me to name the civil servants I had in mind. I issued a press statement which was published in the 'Daily Nation' of Friday 21st Jan 1994. However, the newspapers did not publish the names of the land grabbers that I had mentioned. These were: Joseph Mengich, a former D.C Kirinyaga; and Mr Pius Kibweett Seurey, a former District Special Branch officer. Each of these had grabbed 10 acres which was supposed to be given to Kandongu people as compensation. I had also mentioned Mr Francis Tilitei, a former District Commissioner, and my challenger, Francis Sigei himself, who was at the centre of the sixty acres land sale scandal.

On Monday 24th January 1994, Mr Josphat Kinyua, the new owner of Jeremiah Kamau's two-acre land came with six men and put up a wooden house and roofed it with iron sheets. They were to fix doors and windows the following day but were stopped short when more than 200 infuriated young people from the two villages visited the site and uprooted the house. They rolled it over several times and left it with the roof upside down. After this they attempted, without much success, to burn the house but the wood was still wet. After this incident, none of the new owners of the plots dared to come and build. The community seems to have become sensitized to the extent that they are no longer going to be mere spectators of injustices perpetrated in their very backyard.

On Monday 11th April, Mr Victor Musoga, the Provincial Commissioner Central Province, paid an official visit to Mwea and held a public meeting at

Kimbimbi. After hearing the cries of people whose land had been grabbed, the P.C publicly nullified the allocation of the sixty acres to seventeen people. Full of joy at this welcome turn of events, the people gave the P.C an ululating applause. Apparently excited by this applause the P.C proceeded to attack the Bishop and further issued a summons, that the Bishop must go the nearest police station and record a statement, giving names of the civil servants he was alleging had grabbed land, and that if he failed to do this he would be arrested. The following day (12th April 1994) the newspapers reported what the P.C had said. I did not go to the police station as Mr Musoga had demanded, as I had already issued a full statement on land-grabbing in Kirinyaga to a commission appointed by Musoga himself. I waited in my house at Difathas for those who would come to arrest me but none turned up except the District Criminal Investigation (CID) officer. We had a friendly chat, after which I gave him the press release I had issued earlier, stating that I was not going to give a statement to the police. The officer accepted the statement and departed with satisfaction.

On Friday 15th April, the Standard published a story stating that

> *'The Central Provincial Commissioner, Mr Victor Musoga, yesterday said Bishop David Gitari of the Church of the Province of Kenya will be taken care of for defying P.C's order to record a statement detailing the alleged involvement by Provincial administration in shoddy land deals in Mwea irrigation scheme.'*

The following Sunday, 18th April 1994, eighty priests from the Diocese of Kirinyaga issued a statement asking the P.C to clarify what he meant by the statement that the Bishop 'will be taken care of'. The clergy warned that if any misfortune befell the Bishop, the P.C would be held as the highest suspect. The P.C responded angrily and dismissed us as unchristian! The confrontation between me and the P.C seemed to have come to an abrupt end until mid-September 1994 when Henry Njeru, the rural dean of Mwea, once again alerted me that 200 acres of land given by the National Irrigation Board (N.I.B) to the Kenya Agricultural Research Institute (KARI) in Mwea was being grabbed by civil servants to compensate the 17 people who had been allocated the 60 acres of Red Soil land (referred to earlier), which was subsequently nullified by the P.C. The rural dean also informed me that the land was being allocated to influencial politicians and civil servants who were in turn selling to tycoons. From mid-September to October 1994 I preached against the grabbing of KARI land and excerpts of my sermons were often carried in the Standard newspaper.

On Monday 25th October 1994, the P.C visited Kirinyaga to install the new Chiefs of Kabare and Njukiini locations. In his speech at Ngekenyi near Kabare, the P.C is reported to have said that the 200 acre land I was talking about was non-existent. He challenged me to come out publicly and show where the land I was talking about was located.On Friday the 21st October 1994 I issued a press statement accepting the P.C's challenge and I informed him that I would be available on Tuesday 1st Nov. 1994 to show him the land, and that I would arrive at the venue, St Barnabas Church Mathangauta, six kilometres from Kimbimbi, at 11am and after conducting prayers in commemoration of All Saints, I would then take the P.C on a tour of the land.When I arrived at the said venue on the appointed day together with my clergy, we found about 2000 people waiting for us but the P.C was nowhere to be seen.

After prayers I led a 6Km procession around the 200 acres. 160 acres have already been given out and only 40 acres is left. It is most likely that among the beneficiaries is the P.C himself and other civil servants under him. Our main concern is not that KARI land has been taken away but that it has been given to the least deserving people while there are so many people in Kirinyaga who are landless. The 160 acres should have been allocated to the landless squatters of Githogondo, Kiorugari, Kangaita, Mwambao and others like them. The Struggle Continues!

Bibliography

The Kenya National Anthem.

Taylor, David Bentley, *My Love Must Wait: The Story of Henry Martyn* (London, Inter-varsity Press, 1975).

Shakespeare, William, *Macbeth.*

King, Martin Luther, *Strength To Love* (Fontana Religious Press).

Report of the Lausanne Congress, 1974.

The Kenya Constitution.

Barclay, William, *The Daily Study Bible on the Gospel of Matthew.*

Barclay, William, *The Daily Study Bible on the Gospel of Mark.*

Barclay, William, *The Daily Study Bible on the Gospel of Luke.*

Barclay, William, *The Daily Study Bible on the Gospel of John.*

Barclay, William, *The Daily Study Bible on the Gospel of Acts of the Apostles.*

Barclay, William, *The Daily Study Bible on the Gospel of Romans.*

Barclay, William, *The Daily Study Bible on the Gospel of James and 1 Peter.*

Baldwin, Joyce, Daniel, *An Introduction and Commentary. Tyndale Old Testament Commentaries* (Inter-varsity Press, 1978).

Gitari, David M., *Let The Bishop Speak.*

Anderson, Bernhard W., *The Living World of The Old Testament* (Longman, 1958).

Wright, Christopher J.H., *God's People in God's Land* (Paternoster Press, 1990).

Richardson, Alan, *Genesis 1–11: The Creation stories and the Modern World View* (Torch Bible Paperbacks. SCM Press Ltd., 1953).

Kidner, Derek, *Genesis, Tyndale Old Testament Commentaries* (Tyndale Press, 1967).

Harrison, R.K., *Old Testament Times* (Inter-varsity Press, 1971).

Harrison, R.K., *Jeremiah and Lamentations, An Introduction and Commentary* (The Tyndale Press, April 1973).

Taylor, John B., *Ezekiel, An Introduction and Commentary* (Tyndale Press, September, 1969).

Church, Leslie F. (Ed.), *Matthew Henry's Commentary on the whole Bible in one volume* (Marshall, Morgan and Scott, Ltd., 1960).

Report of the Kanu Review Committee presented to His Excellency Hon. Daniel T. Arap Moi, C.G.H., M.P. President and Commander-in-Chief of the Armed Forces of the Republic of Kenya and President of the ruling party, Kanu, by the Chairman Hon. Prof. George Saitoti, E.G.H., M.P. Vice President and Minister for Finance, October, 1990.

Samuel, Vinay and Sugden, Chris, (eds), *The Church in Response to Human Need* (Regnum Books, Paternoster Press, 1987).
Beyond Magazine, (banned by the government since March, 1988). (Publishers: The National Council of Churches of Kenya, February, 1988).
Kirinyaga County Council Minutes of 19th February, 1991.
DeWitt, Calvin, *Take Care, it's God's Earth*: an article in *Prism Magazine* (Dec/Jan. 1994).
Kidner, Derek Rev., *Psalms 73–150, Tyndale Old Testament Commentaries* (Inter-varsity Press, 1975).
Standard Newspaper (7th June, 1991).
Pink, A.W., *The Life of Elijah* (The Banner of Truth Trust, 1968).